Ask the Wine Whisperer: All the wine wisdom you need to flabbergast your friends, astound your associates, amaze your acquaintances, and dumbfound your dates.

For information contact:
Creative Projects International Inc.
4001 Santa Barbara Blvd.,
Suite 404,
Naples,
Florida 34104

ISBN-978-0-9818222-8-0
Library of Congress Control Number: 2018954002

Design & Typography: www.JimandZetta.com
Cover Design: Katherine Warden Designs

ASK THE WINE WHISPERER!

All the wine wisdom you need to
flabbergast your friends,
astound your associates,
amaze your acquaintances,
and dumbfound your dates.

Jerry Greenfield
The Wine Whisperer™

Also by Jerold A. Greenfield

Maverick – The Personal War of a Vietnam Cobra Pilot
with Dennis J. Marvicsin

Secrets of the Wine Whisperer
Or
How I Learned to Drink Wine
and Found Ecstasy, Joy, Peace,
Happiness, Life, and Salvation

DASPO – An Unhinged Novel of Vietnam
with Ronald B. Fenster

Dedication

In my first wine book, *Secrets of the Wine Whisperer,* I told the story of how my wife Debi and I fell into the wine life. Since then, for the past 20 years or so, we have both delighted in the surprises and pleasures that our love for wine (and each other) has brought us. The travel. The flavorful discoveries. Most of all, the wonderful friends.

I've become a wine columnist, the Wine Director of an international wine club, and an adjunct professor, teaching a wine course at a university. This is not a journey I would have enjoyed nearly as much had I taken it alone. And I could not think of a better traveling companion than Debi. She has a discriminating palate, a terrific sense of smell, an everlasting impulse to travel, and best of all, tremendous tolerance for my craziness.

This is for her.

TABLE OF CONTENTS

All the Wine Wisdom You Need to Flabbergast Your Friends, Astound Your
Associates, Amaze Your Acquaintances, and Dumbfound Your Dates.

Introduction

For several years, I've been fortunate enough to be a
wine writer and educator. My columns appear in
weekly and monthly publications, and quite a few of
them have piled up.

As I looked over the topics I've covered – the wine
grapes, the places they're grown, and the people who
actually make wine – it occurred to me that if I put
them all together, they'd collectively form a pretty
decent overview of the wine world itself. Not a
comprehensive one, by any means: there are dozens of
books a lot thicker and heavier that try to do that,
mostly with a good deal of success. For example, *The
Oxford Encyclopedia of Wine* is just what it says -- an
encyclopedia. And it weighs a ton, because it contains
a ton of information.

One of my favorite wine writers is Andrea Immer
Robinson, whom I've been lucky enough to meet. In
one of her books about the basics of wine she divides
the topic into three parts. If you want to get
pretentious about it, they are the vine, the vineyard,
and the vintner. I prefer a more down to earth
approach, so I just write about the grapes, the ground,
and the guy or gal who makes the wine.

So that's the way I've organized this collection. The first part covers (to a moderate extent) some of my favorite wine grapes, what they are, and their flavor profiles. The second part is about the ground – the major winegrowing regions of the world and what makes them so special. The third is a compilation of interviews and articles I've done about winemakers who bring their own special touch, and special life story, to the art and science of making wine. The fourth section, quite frankly, is a series of articles that I just couldn't classify. They deal with the wine world at large, musing on topics that don't easily fall into any special category.

In Part V I share some thoughts, musings, and ruminations about wine and women. At one time, wine was considered pretty much of a "guy thing," but not anymore. Many quite famous winemakers and winery owners are women, and they're crafting bottles that sell for hundreds of dollars. To finish up, the last section is a sort of FAQ...issues that have been brought to my attention by readers over the years. The questions wander all through the world of wine, and I hope my responses will inform you and help satisfy your curiosity.

Overall, I think this book would be a good start for beginning wine enthusiasts, and also for those who are a bit further along in the wine life. Perhaps you have 50-100 bottles in a small refrigerator, or in boxes at the bottom of a closet. Or maybe the whole wine buying thing is starting to get out of hand, and you've graduated to a 200 bottle stand-alone wine cabinet. The next step is to sell one of the children and convert their room into a refrigerated custom wine cellar. But be careful. When we built ours, we were warned that when you build a wine cellar, you double your collection in a year.

That's what happened to us, though we didn't have to sell the kids. I hope you enjoy these brief essays...and I hope you double your collection.

All the Wine Wisdom You Need to Flabbergast Your Friends, Astound Your Associates, Amaze Your Acquaintances, and Dumbfound Your Dates.

PART I
THE GRAPES

*W*hen you come right down to it, wine is nothing but grape juice that went bad. But it spoils in the most delightful and different way. People make wine from hundreds of different varieties of grapes. Here's an introduction to some of our favorites.

This section deals with some, though certainly not all, the grapes used to make wine throughout the world. I have a chart of the world's wine grapes on my office wall. There are over 200 of them, ranging from Airén through Lladoner Pelut to Zinfandel. Admittedly, many of them are blending grapes and you'd never see their names on a bottle label. Others are severely local, and seldom leave the regions where they're grown.

Still, many of the major varietals are represented – the ones you're most likely to find on the shelf. Hope it helps.

Grab a Cab

Every year, the wine industry, like many industries, stages an expo for the trade. The one for worldwide wine producers, retailers, wholesalers, and others in the biz is called VinExpo. In alternate years, it's held in (surprise) Bordeaux, and then someplace in the Orient, like Hong Kong or Japan.

Aside from the obvious attraction and fun of the event, when you spend a solid week sampling wines (don't ask) from every region where grapes can be grown, you just have to get a better understanding of why some varietals are so universally popular, and why some are, at best, an acquired taste.

Which brings me to Cabernet Sauvignon, especially those from California. There's good news and bad news.

As anyone who has traveled to the Napa area knows, the noble Cabernet is the king of the region. And ever since the early 1970s California Cabernets have set the bar for world class winemaking. The bad news, of course, is that many of the premium labels have become so expensive. Not as expensive, of course, as the wines from the premium chateaux in Bordeaux: the latest releases from that area are asking (and getting) prices in the $1,200-a-bottle range.

But still, not cheap. The best known brands, such as Phelps Insignia, or Opus One (originally made as a cooperative effort between Robert Mondavi and Baron Eric de Rothschild) will run you about $175 a bottle. And the so-called "cult" Cabernets like Harlan Estate or Screaming Eagle go for $750 a pop, if you can get them. In general, for a top-end Cabernet from the Napa region, you can plan on spending upwards of a C-note.

Now for the good news. There are still California Cabernets that offer the classic flavor profile of cassis, blackberry, blueberry, plum, toasty oak, spice, vanilla, cocoa, and sometimes an undertone of eucalyptus or mint. And best of all, some of them are grown right next door to the big names, in districts like Diamond Mountain, Spring Mountain, and Rutherford.

It's a bit surprising that this varietal is a relative newcomer on the wine scene. A cross between Cabernet Franc and Sauvignon Blanc, it appeared around the end of the 18th century, and gained instant popularity. What is it about Cabernet Sauvignon that makes it so appealing, that impels winemakers to grow it all over the world? The flavors and aromas, of course, but also the fact that it has a big, bold structure, thanks to the tannins in the skins and stems, and that it very well reflects the characteristics of the region where it's grown. If you sampled three Cabernets side by side, one from Chile, say, one from California, and one from France, you may not be able to tell which one comes from which country, but the differences among them would still be unmistakable.

So…where to find great Cabernets that won't cost a car payment? Rule Number One is to look for wines from lesser-known regions. Wines from Napa Valley's Diamond Mountain can be pricey, so look on the Sonoma side of the mountains instead…to Alexander Valley, Russian River, Mendocino, and Dry Creek. Amador County, the home of the Gold Rush, is a bit out of the way, but offers great values.

Rule Number Two is to consider the second labels from the top wineries. Every premium winery carefully selects the grapes that are used in the top brand. The bunches that don't quite make the cut go into a second label, which can still be not only quite good, but an excellent value as well. When you start to pursue – and appreciate – this premium varietal, a little shopping around and comparative sampling can lead you to great values.

Fizzies, Flutes, and Holiday Wines

Every year, people starting wondering and stressing about what kind of wine to serve with traditional holiday repasts. Holiday meals contain such a wide range of flavors and textures that pairing becomes a real problem.

My choice has always been sparkling whites – especially Champagne. For me, this particular wine goes with everything, and it doesn't have to be expensive.

Champagnes offer a very wide range of choices. Legally, the wine must come from the designated Champagne region of France. However, sparkling whites from other places might say "méthode traditionelle" or "méthode champenoise," which means that they're made according to the procedure used in Champagne. It is very complex, involving the blending of up to 40 or 50 separate still wines (Chardonnay, Pinot Noir, and Pinot Meuniere) to achieve a house style, then fermenting them a second time in the bottle so that the released carbon dioxide goes into the liquid and makes the bubbles. There's lots more to this particular procedure, but you might find any further explanation to be snooze-inducing. Many people who make still wines feel that their task is to get the grapes from the vine into the bottle with as little interference and manipulation as possible, but Champagne is one of the most manipulated wines you can buy. This is not necessarily a bad thing.

A bit of terminology is helpful to know. Sparkling wines are classified by sweetness and by the composition of the blend. So "brut" is a dry wine made from blending the three grapes mentioned above. "Blanc de blancs" is made from 100% Chardonnay, "Blanc de Noirs" from all Pinot Noir, and rosé from a blend of the white and red wines.

If it says "brut" on the label, it is the driest wine, with the least sugar. Then in order of increasing sugar content, comes "extra sec," "sec," "demi-sec," and "doux," which is the sweetest. I'd recommend the brut to accompany most holiday meals.

After you bring them home, there's lots more to do. First, you have to pull the cork. Forget what you see in the movies or sports team victory celebrations where the cork flies out of the bottle and foam explodes all over the party guests. There's more pressure in a Champagne bottle than in a car tire and a flying cork can do some real damage. Remove the wire cage while holding your thumb on the cork, put a towel around the neck, hold the cork and twist the bottle.

About the vessel you're going to drink out of. You're not going to use milady's slipper and you're not going to use one of those broad cup-like glasses they trot out at weddings that are supposed to be modeled after Marie Antoinette's breast. You're also not going to use a traditional flute. Why? Because professional Champagne people prefer white wine glasses, like the ones you'd use for Chardonnay.

We were invited to a a private tasting in New York where Cyril Brun, the *chef de cave* at the world famous Charles Heidsieck house, explained it to us thusly: "Flutes tend to emphasize the bubbles, while a Chardonnay glass emphasizes the aromas and flavors." Good enough for me.

The Pleasures – and Perils – of Pinot Noir

Winemakers who decide to try their hands at making Pinot Noir are crazy in a very special way, because Pinot is known far and wide as the "heartbreak grape." Unlike Chardonnay, which will grow just about anywhere you stick it in the ground, Pinot thrives only in a narrow range of soil and climate conditions. Second, the grapes themselves are very small, so it takes more of them to make a bottle of wine. Third, if wine grapes can get any disease or malady at all, Pinot grapes will catch it first. And if that's not discouraging enough, the varietal is known to actually mutate on the vine, so what you plant may not be what you harvest.

But there's an upside. Of all grapes, Pinot Noir is capable of being turned into wines that are surpassingly elegant, silky, and seductive. Which is why a Pinot such as France's Domaine de la Romanée Conti sells for somewhere between $3,500 and $12,000 a bottle, if you can find it. (A double magnum of the 1996 vintage can be yours for a mere $69,995). Pinot is thus an attractive challenge for the winemaker, who, if successful, can create a truly spectacular wine that sells for large dollars.

So if Pinot Noir grows well in only very limited areas, where are they? The first, of course, is the Burgundy region in France. Over there, they grow only two grapes: Chardonnay and Pinot Noir, and they are mostly spectacular. They are also supremely difficult to understand, because Burgundy is divided up into miniscule subregions, each of which has its own vineyard name, village name, character, and winemaking traditions. On the other hand, reasonably-priced wines are available, if you choose from some of the lesser-known areas, such as the Macon region, Rully, and Vire Clesse.

Here in the US, Pinot lovers turn to Oregon and California. The most familiar area in Oregon is the Willamette Valley (it's "Wil-AM-it," dammit!) though don't be afraid to sample from the Umpqua and Rogue Valleys as well.

Just as Robert Mondavi put California wines on the world stage, David Lett did the same for the wines of Oregon. In 1979, at an international wine tasting competition, his Eyrie Vineyard Pinot Noir came in third among 600 wines, beating out a whole lineup of legendary and obscenely expensive Burgundies. It was like the American Olympic hockey team defeating the Russians in 1980. Or the 1969 New York Mets.

The French went, bananas, or *bananes,* the way they say it. They exclaimed, "*Sacre bleu! C'est imposible!*" or words to that effect. They absolutely could not accept that an *American* wine could compare so favorably to the best of Burgundy. So they demanded a rematch. A second blind tasting competition was held the next year under identical conditions, staged by Robert Drouhin, one of the most legendary figures in Burgundian winemaking. Eyrie Vineyard Pinot Noir did not come in third. It came in second.

Robert Drouhin immediately went to Oregon and bought as many vineyards as he could get his hands on.

Pinots tend to be extremely variable in quality and style, so the best way to get started with them is to select your wines by producer. Sample widely (of course), find a few producers you like, and stick with them.

White Nights

According to conventional wisdom, summer is the time to sip light white wines, and winter is supposed to be when we break out the big reds. Well, maybe I don't have any wisdom, conventional or otherwise, but we like to drink whites in the winter, too.

First, we live in Southwest Florida, so it doesn't get all that cold and we still unwind out on the patio after work in the so-called winter months. At those times, reds are just a bit too big for the balmy weather. Second, we find it especially relaxing to have a glass of white just after work while we're deciding which red to pair with dinner.

And another thing: not all whites are light and refreshing. Rhône varietals, like Viognier, Roussanne, and Marsanne, have a lot of body to them, lower acidity, and bold floral and fruit aromas. These require a whole different food pairing strategy.

There are other reasons to keep the whites in mind during the cooler months. First, it's stone crab season, and there's nothing like a bottle (or two) of zingy Sauvignon Blanc to accompany a heap of claws with butter and mustard sauce. And we still eat fish and other shellfish during that time of year, so it's a good idea to have a collection of Chardonnays, Chenin Blancs, and other varietals within easy reach.

Don't hesitate a minute to try other, less familiar varietals as well, like a zingy Falanghina from Campania in southern Italy. Other less-common whites, such as Aligote and Colombard from France's Gascony region, are also great discoveries.

The ABCs of Chardonnay

Favorite grapes, huh? Where to start? Well, before we go off the beaten vineyard path, it might be a good idea to take a fresh look at some of the most famous wine types. In the wine world, as everywhere else, fashions evolve, and styles change. So if you got fed up with, say, those heavily-oaked superbuttery California Chardonnays a few years ago, maybe a sip of the more modern offerings will bring you back. Worked for me.

Chardonnay is the world's favorite white wine, but wines, as I have mentioned, go in and out of fashion. To paraphrase Yogi Berra, "Chardonnay is so popular nobody drinks it anymore." But people drink plenty of it, and the shelves at the wine stores groan under the weight of all the different bottles. Beside, winemakers love this grape because they can make it in an enormous range of styles. Oaky and buttery, lean and minerally, and just about everywhere in between. Best of all, unlike some other wine grapes, it's not all that particular about where you plant it.

In the wine world, certain grapes are classified as "noble varietals." Chardonnay is one of these, because it's capable of gaining elegance, dimension, and layers of complexity as it ages. White Burgundy is an excellent example. Chablis, which is a district of

Burgundy, is another. And Champagne is generally a blend of Chardonnay with other grapes.

A few years ago, wine lovers started yelling, "A-B-C!" Anything But Chardonnay. The reason? Winemakers, mostly in California, had, almost en masse, swung toward a style that was soaked in oak, which pretty much covered up all the other elegant flavors that this grape is capable of delivering. But later, the style came back in the other direction, and many Chardonnays deliver a wide range of "tutti-frutti" flavors that make it so much fun.

Why not do a taste test, and find out for yourself? For example, ask your favorite wine store person for a bottle each of unoaked and oaked Chardonnay. The unoaked will be clean and minerally, with a nice zippy acidity on the palate. The oaked version will be much richer on the nose, and the aroma of oak will be unmistakable. On the palate, there's a buttery feel, a mouthfilling weight to the wine that's both very pleasant and very different from the unoaked style. Each has its fans, and each can be paired with a wide variety of cheeses and other foods.

Since there are so many Chardonnay styles, a stroll off the beaten track can provide some tasty new discoveries, and not always at the price of a new BMW. Bargains can be had.

Don't ever be shy about trying new wines from new places. The Chileans are making some very fine examples, as are the South Africans. And even in Burgundy, there are some excellent Chardonnays available for under $30 a bottle. The key to

discovering new wines and learning about them?
Sampling widely.

Merlot -- The Best Wine
You're Not Drinking

In the wine business, it's called the "Sideways
Effect." It refers to the astounding decline in sales of
Merlot resulting from what happened in the 2004
sleeper hit movie "Sideways." If you're one of the very
few wine lovers who has not seen it, here's a brief
summary.

Miles and Jack, two old college buddies now in their
maybe thirties, go up to wine country north of Santa
Barbara for a week of golf and wine sampling. At one
point, Jack suggests they have a glass of Merlot, and
Miles, who is something of a wine geek, famously
declares, "If anyone orders Merlot, I'm leaving. I am
not drinking any %&*!@#$ Merlot!"

Long story short, the whole market for Merlot tanked
practically overnight, although industry insiders have
said this particular varietal had started to slide a few
years earlier. Anyway, it has yet to fully recover, and
that's a shame. Some people call Merlot the best wine
you're not drinking.

First of all, many of the world's most famous (and
most expensive) wines are made from the Merlot
grape, or have a good splash of Merlot blended in. In
the Pomerol area of Bordeaux, Chateau Petrus, which
will cost you around $6,000 a bottle for a decent
vintage, is almost 100% Merlot. A more reasonably
priced alternative at around $40 is Chateau Nenin,

from the same Bordeaux region, which is about 80% Merlot and the rest Cabernet Franc. Other well-known wines from the same area contain a higher percentage of Merlot than anything else.

And if that's not enough, *Wine Spectator* magazine named California's Paloma Merlot as #1 Wine of the Year in 2003.

I like to think of Merlot as the "twin cousin" of Cabernet Sauvignon, because it has the same flavor profile. You'll notice that signature cassis or black currant flavor, plus blackberries and other dark fruits. The good thing is that it's less tannic, rounder and plusher. That makes it a perfect blending partner. Most winemakers mix Merlot in with their Cabernet Sauvignon to soften the tannins of the latter wine, and make it easier to drink young.

It's especially appealing because it's right down the middle in terms of taste, body, and color – about halfway between a Pinot Noir and a Syrah. There's a lot of variety to it, as well. Merlots from cooler climates, like France, Chile, and Italy, are full-bodied and generally more tannic. From places like California and Australia, expect softer tannins, raspberry, juicy cherry, and spices like clove and nutmeg.

Plus, it's the most-planted grape in France, so somebody somewhere must like it.

The Resurgence of Rosé

In a way, wines styles are like skirt hemlines. They're up, they're down, in fashion and out of fashion. One day everybody's drinking Chenin Blanc, and a few months later it's all Pinot Grigio.

Rosé wines are sort of like that. They were extremely popular in the mid-1950s and have come back strong, partly because that's just the way things work, but mostly because new offerings come onto the market, providing wine lovers (that's us) with interesting and unique flavors and sensations. After all, Brad Pitt and Angelina Jolie spent $60 million to buy a vineyard in France just to make rosé wines, so how bad can the stuff be?

Unfortunately, the pink wine that most readily comes to mind for most of us is the inevitable and regrettable low-alcohol white Zinfandel. In 2014, over 7.7 million cases of the sweetish swill were sold in the US (less than previous years) but it's still a biggie. However, we're interested in more serious liquids.

When summer comes, it's not a bad idea to turn to rosés as our first sipping solution. For picnic purposes, we can forsake the traditional Pinot Grigio and enjoy the many rosé wines on the shelf that give us bright refreshing flavors, plus a really pretty pink liquid to look at while we sip.

First of all, there are two ways to make rosé wines. You can mix a white and red together. Indeed, many big red wines contain a percentage of white, like Australian Shiraz, which is often enhanced by about 5% of Viognier, a white grape. And pink Champagne-style wines are made exactly that way: red and white make pink. The second, more legitimate way, is the *saignee* method. You crush red grapes, leave the juice on the skins until it turns the pink color you want, then drain it off. It's more expensive, but many in the wine world believe that it's a more "legitimate" way to make rosé. So that's the kind we'll discuss here.

Rosé can be made from just about any red grape. It is also made in an incredibly wide range of styles because it's entirely the winemaker's choice as to how long the juice stays on the skins, how dark it gets, and when it's drained away. That's why it's critical to drink a lot of wine, to sample widely, and find producers who make wine in a style you enjoy.

In a way, the spiritual home of rosé wine as a specific type is the area around Tavel and Lirac in Provence. These are tiny areas, just north of Avignon, and Tavel is the only appellation in the Rhône that produces rosé wines exclusively. The rosés in this area are based primarily on Grenache and Syrah, but tradition allows several other grapes as minor components of the blend. In other parts of the world, as mentioned above, just about any red grape can be used.

The flavors of rosé wines are traditionally light, because it's long-term contact with the skins that makes red wine big and bold. But that's okay, because these delicate flavors are perfect not only for summer sipping, but also for pairing with a wide range of foods and cheeses. The flavor profiles will be the same as the major grape in the blend, but lighter and more delicate.

There's Nothing Petite
About Petite Sirah

As I've already observed, wines go in and out of style. One day everybody's going mad over Malbec, and three months later they're crazy for Chenin Blanc. As I write this Petite Sirah is enjoying a well-deserved upsurge in buzz...and in popularity.

Known as Durif in other parts of the world, it was planted in California as early as 1884, and was popular during Prohibition, because it has a very thick skin, which allowed the fruit to hold up well when shipped across the country to the "home winemakers." Traditionally, it has been used as a blending grape, because it imparts rich color and tannic structure. While many vintners are bottling it as a single varietal, it's not uncommon for them to add a bit of white wine to calm it down. Today, there are about 6,000 acres of Petite Sirah planted in California, with dozens of winemakers trying their hand at the varietal.

As mentioned, you can expect this wine to offer deep, opaque coloration and rich, bold flavors. Typically, you'll find dark berry and plum fruit, black pepper and similar spices. While it's not one of the "noble" varietals like Cabernet Sauvignon or Pinot Noir, it can be delicious... especially if you like big, rich wines. If you're collecting, you can probably put this in your cellar for several years, because of the bold structure.

Solving the Prosecco Puzzle

As Yul Brynner said way back when in *The King and I,* "It's a puzzlement." The puzzle is why we insist on saving our enjoyment of Champagnes and other sparkling wines for special occasions. Of course, many of them are a bit expensive, and we've all seen victorious sports teams celebrating their championships by dousing the coach with it and spraying it all over the locker room. But still...

There are tons of excellent sparkling wines from all over the world that can – and should – be enjoyed on a much more regular basis. First of all, they're not overly expensive, and second, they pair really well with a wide variety of cuisines. There are sparkling whites and rosés from the US made with the same process used in Champagne. There's Cava from Spain, Sekt from Germany, Cremant from Alsace and other regions...and then there's Prosecco.

This sparkler is made mainly in the Valdobbiadene region, around the hill town of Conigliano, just north and a bit west of Venice. As you'd expect, it's fairly close to the mountains, the climate is cooler, so the area is perfect for growing the acidic white grapes ideal for sparkling wines. The main grape is called Glera. Often, producers will throw in a little Pinot Bianco or Pinot Grigio.

Unlike Champagne, the bubbles are produced by the Charmat method, which involves fermenting the crushed grapes in tightly sealed stainless steel tanks. Since the CO_2 released by the fermentation can't escape, it goes back into the liquid and creates the carbonation. As you may expect, it's a less expensive production method than the complex and time-consuming process used in Champagne-style wines.

But that's okay, because most Prosecco is dry and lemony; the flavors and enjoyment are very much there, and they span a wide range of styles. With Prosecco, there's something for everyone to like.

Are There Bargains in Bordeaux?

For many years, the prices for the higher-level wines from Bordeaux have shot into the stratosphere. A wine like the famous Lafite Rothschild used to cost around $220 on release. Today it's upwards of a grand. Or more.

A lot of the price ridiculousness is the result of increasing prosperity in other areas of the world, especially China. There are tons of new millionaires who want only "the best" and don't care how much it costs. That puts you and I pretty well out of the market. But, like you, I'm always on the lookout for wines that still offer the classic Bordeaux experience but won't cost as much as a condo on the beach. Of course, I've had to sample dozens and dozens of wines to accomplish this, but you know what they say about dirty jobs.

First, let's review some basics. The red wines of Bordeaux are actually blends of up to five different grapes: Cabernet Sauvignon, Merlot, Petit Verdot, Cabernet Franc, and Malbec. The tradition of blending these grapes together goes back hundreds of years. Depending on where in the region the winemaker is located, either Cabernet Sauvignon or Merlot will dominate the blend. That makes a difference, and we'll see why in a minute.

Second, the chateaux (wine estates) in this area are classified in a bunch of different ways. The most famous is the classification done by the French government in 1855 that divided 61 estates on the Left Bank (east and south of the Gironde river) into five categories, known as "crus," or "growths." First growth, second growth, and so on. This classification has been revised only once since it was devised over 150 years ago, so some of the chateaux that received a low classification way back when might have improved over the last century and a half. Similarly, some of the higher rated estates may have declined. C'est la vie.

Obviously, most of the wines from these "classified growth" producers will tend to be a bit on the pricey side. Not all, but most. So the trick is to look for classifications that may be a bit less well known, but still have the earthy, sumptuous, elegant character we expect from this region's wines.

One classification that's been getting my attention is called *Cru Bourgeois*. All the producers are located in the Medoc, in eight appellations on the left bank of the Gironde River, which divides the Bordeaux region about in half. The classification Cru Bourgeois has been revised several times, and today lists 243 wines, so there's a lot of choice and variety. And the producers themselves have formed a kind of trade association or alliance with a new logo and everything, to promote the specific classification and their wines in the world market. They formed an independent committee to conduct the assessment of the wines, and to make sure production standards are met. Then, winemakers submitted their bottles to a blind tasting panel for final evaluation.

The other interesting aspect about this designation is that winemakers must submit their wines to the panel each year to be judged for quality, and they either make the cut or they don't. So, unlike the 1855 Classification, no winery is permanently on the list.

In addition to *Cru Bourgeois,* there is a classification called *Bordeaux Superior,* which is also worth seeking out. So don't worry about those thousand-dollar First Growths, unless you're celebrating becoming a dot-com billionaire. There's a lot more to Bordeaux that's well worth a try.

Zinfandel – The Mystery Wine

One of the really interesting things about Zinfandel is that until recently, nobody knew where the grape came from. It grows almost exclusively in California, and has since the middle of the 19th Century. But it had to come from…somewhere.

Now, thanks to the science of ampellography, which performs DNA analysis on wine grape varietals, we know that Zinfandel grapes originally came from Croatia (of all places) and has a genetic twin in the Primitivo grape, which is grown mostly in Apulia, the heel of the Italian boot.

American Zinfandel comes from cuttings brought to the US from Austria back around 1820, and was the favorite wine of the 49ers in the Gold Rush days. In fact, most of the original Zinfandel vines (which are very old) are planted in Amador County, which was one of the centers of Gold Rush fever. Many vines are up to 75 or 100 years old and still producing today, which is why you may see the phrase "old vines" or "ancient vines" on the label.

In spite of the fact that it can be terrific to enjoy, Zinfandel is not considered a "serious" wine. It's best consumed within three to five years of the vintage because the big fruit flavors we love diminish over time and the alcohol content becomes more obvious. So we don't cellar a Zin for 20 or 30 years as we would a big Bordeaux or Cabernet. Further lack of respect comes from its use as a major component of California jug wines like "hearty Burgundy," and it was a favorite grape of home winemakers during Prohibition. It's also used to make so-called "white Zinfandel," which is the ultrasweet, pinkish fruity stuff that has been so popular from the 1980s to today. There is no such grape as white Zinfandel. I repeat: no such grape.

Stylistically, Zinfandel stands alone. We expect a certain taste experience when we enjoy wines from Bordeaux, the Rhone, Burgundy and similar historic places, but Zinfandel has no such heritage. As a result, it's available in a wide range of styles, from light and fruity like Beaujolais to rich and extracted like Cabernet. There are even late harvest styles that taste much like Port.

I call Zinfandel "America's wine" because (A) most people consider it indigenous to California, (B) because it's not grown very much outside the US, and (C) because there's no better wine to drink with your backyard barbecue. It's perfect with grilled and stewed meats, and just the right accent to sweet and smoky sauces.

In fact, ZAP, the Zinfandel Advocates and Producers trade group, calls it our "Heritage Wine."

Another thing to know about Zinfandel is that its characteristic lush extracted fruit flavors support very high levels of alcohol. You can drink a Zin that has over 15% alcohol and not know it…until it's maybe too late.

Even though some people like to say that the best Zinfandels come from wineries that begin with the letter "R," like Rosenblum, Renwood, Ravenswood, Ridge, and Rafanelli, there are plenty of easy-drinking, food-friendly examples on the shelf. They're attractive for their aromas of violets and rose petal, and big jammy fruit flavors of black cherry, strawberry, cranberry, and raspberry. There's usually some cinnamon, clove, and vanilla in there as well. What's not to like?

Gewürz Gains Ground

This tonguetwister grape has always been one of our favorites with Indian food, so when I was invited to a sampling with some professionals from the wine trade, I broke out our special Helicium tasting glasses with utmost speed.

We normally associate Gewürztraminer, a cool-weather white grape, with the Alsace region between France and Germany, but some other regions are trying their hands at it, too. This grape needs to be grown very far north (or south) because cold weather is critical. That means places like Washington State, maybe Canada, and the very southern parts of New Zealand, among a few others.

Italy's Alto Adige region is getting into the Gewürz game. The area is so far north and borders so closely on Germany it's barely in Italy at all. Up there, many winemakers vinify this grape in a wide range of styles, producing a lot of excellent sweet wine. Our preference, though, is for a drier, leaner style, with the classic characteristics of cream, spice, lychee, and citrus.

Most of the drier styles offer aromas and flavors of honey, white flowers, and green apple supported by bracing acidity.

If you like sweet wines, look for bottles labeled *vendage tardive* (late harvest) or *passito.* But the drier styles are more suitable as complements to food, especially highly aromatic cuisines such as Indian or Thai. Even if it's not summertime, any time is the right time to enjoy this pleasant varietal.

Weird Whites

Like most things, wines go in and out of style. For a long time (and still today) Chardonnay is extremely popular. But once in a while a wine like Pinot Grigio gets a buzz, and restaurants' by-the-glass sales of that particular wine start to skyrocket. Nobody knows why this happens.

Well, here's some good news. There is life beyond Chardonnay and Pinot Grigio, and enjoying the whites that are a bit off the beaten vineyard track requires only a slight bit of adventurousness on your part.

Of course, right up there in the white wine department is Sauvignon Blanc. The good news is that there are stunningly wonderful Sauvignon Blancs available in the under $20 range...some New Zealand delights go for as low as $12 or $13. And then there are examples from Sancerre and Pouilly in the Loire Valley that can set you back $100 a bottle. Many of them are worth every nickel.

But what about those....*other* white wines? The ones you seldom see on the shelves, and if you did see them, you'd have a hard time recognizing the names. Well, the good news is that the lesser-known varietals offer incredible bargains, mostly because they're kind of obscure, and perhaps come from relatively unknown winegrowing regions.

One fairly popular grape is Viognier (Vee-on-YAY), which is now grown well outside its native France. In fact, the Australians have taken it to heart, and when they're not blending it with Shiraz (a common practice) they bottle it as a single varietal. Yalumba also makes a white called Vermentino. Mainly cultivated in Italy, it's a refreshing, fun wine, not terribly serious, offering apple, peach, lemon, and mineral flavors. It's available on local shelves, so if you see a bottle somewhere, it's worth a try.

Another recent favorite is a Greek white called Moschofilero (that's mos-ko-FEE-le-ro). One of the best producers of this newly-popular wine is Boutari. Their white offers lovely floral aromas, and bracing acidity.

In Spain, the wine to try is Verdejo. This grape is also grown in Australia, of all places, and **Mollydooker The Violinist** is a great and tasting example. The reds and whites of legendary Spanish producer Marques de Riscal are some big favorites, and their version offers flavors of nectarine, peach, and stone fruit. Besides, their new winery in the Rioja region is a breathtaking architectural triumph.

A recent discovery is a white from the southern Rhône valley in France. It was a real surprise, because the Rhône is famous for big, savory reds blended from Syrah, Grenache, and Mourvedre, with some other reds and whites thrown in. But the **Pierre Henri Morel Laudon Cotes du Rhône Villages** was a huge revelation. First, because whites from the southern Rhône are very rare, and second because it's not made from the traditional white grapes of the area.

Normally, white Rhônes are made from Roussanne and Marsanne, the heritage grapes of the region. But this is a blend of Grenache Blanc and a grape called Bourboulenc. This latter grape can be part of the blend for the famous wines of Châteauneuf du Pape, but it's extremely rare. The Laudon is sort of halfway between a Viognier and a Sauvignon Blanc, with the best qualities of both. Killer stuff.

So…don't wait for summer. Any time is a good time for a refreshing white on a Saturday afternoon. Crank up your adventurous spirit and discover these zippy, refreshing whites.

Malbec Madness

They've been growing Malbec in the south of France since Roman times, and successfully, too. But when the Argentines got their hands on some cuttings and planted them in Mendoza, things really took off. Today, Argentina grows three-quarters of the world's Malbec, and Argentinian wine imports to the US are up over 25%.

So what's the big deal? Well, Malbec is a huge wine -- a jammy rich red that offers rich extracted flavors of plum, blackberry, tobacco, raisins, and coffee. The finer examples also impart briar, and even a bacony note that makes them pair perfectly with all that steak they eat down in Argentina. Second, it's pretty easy to grow, even though it has thin skin and is susceptible to several diseases. That doesn't deter the Argentines, because they grow it at higher altitudes, where the climate is colder and the skins thicken up. It's a vigorous plant, too, producing huge clusters. There are more grapevines in Argentina's Mendoza region than in all of Australia and New Zealand combined.

But many people don't know that the Malbec craze actually started in France...in the southern Cahors region, to be exact, where it was a sort of rustic version of Merlot for hundreds of years. And it was popular as a major blending wine in Bordeaux. Now, not so much.

Too bad, because Cahors wines are delicious, and often great bargains. But when American consumers see the word "Cahors" on the label, and no indication of the fact that it's Malbec, they pass it by. Don't. The (original) French version of this wine is well worth a try. Or two. My personal favorite is **Chateau Labrande,** and it's very reasonably priced. We've already been through a case of it.

Sidebar: before Prohibition, Malbec was widely grown in the US, and used to make bulk wines. But today, the French work closely with winegrowers in Mendoza and other South American regions to grow, promote, and improve their products. And they've succeeded.

Wines You Never Heard Of

How would you like a nice glass of Harslevelu? Never heard of it? You're not alone.

As we've noted before in this space, the world of wine is vast and extensive. There are many countries where wine is made (including China, and much of the wine is better than you'd think) and over 200 varieties of grapes to make it from. The wall chart in my office lists 184 varietals, and that's probably not all of them. In fact, I've been a wine geek for over 20 years, and people will still pull out a bottle of something I've never heard of. That's what makes this all so much fun.

Recently, I received a bottle of Bombino Bianco, which was a bit of a surprise, because we've sipped our way all over Italy, from Sicily to Milan, and had never encountered it. This was a light refreshing white from the "heel" of Italy's boot, and we'll be looking for more of it.

Many wine grapes are obscure, or unknown for many reasons. First is that some are used in wines that never leave their area of production. In the far eastern reaches of France near the Alps, for instance, they make a wine called *vin jaune,* or "yellow wine." It's produced from a grape called Savagnin, which grows only in that region. While the wine is available from several online retailers, I have never seen it on a wine store shelf. And there are many other varietals and regions just like that.

Teroldego makes a really interesting Italian red. And Touriga Nacional is a major component of red table wines from Portugal. The situation is complicated even further by the fact that in the Old World, the wines are known by their place names, and not the name of the grape. So you'd never know that Sherry, which is a place name (in Spanish it's *Jerez*) is made from a grape called Palomino.

Also, many varietals are grown specifically to be used in blends, and are rarely, if ever, bottled all by themselves. Here, good examples would be Petit Verdot, a significant component of the Bordeaux blend, and Tannat, which comes primarily from Southwestern France, but is also grown very successfully in Uruguay (of all places). They can be delicious on their own, but finding them is a bit of a chore.

But when you come right down to it, this is all part of the real enjoyment of discovering wine. There are always new regions, new varietals, and new sensations. So sample widely!

Going Blanc in South Africa

If you happened to stop by the annual Aspen Food & Wine Classic held in mid-June, you might attend a special tasting of Chenin Blanc staged by Wines of South Africa (WOSA), the organization representing all South African wine producers and exporters.

Sadly, not enough beginning (or even advanced) wine enthusiasts know much about this especially delightful white varietal, which is mostly indigenous to the central Loire valley in France. To solve that problem, the Southeast Wine Collective in Oregon set out to promote the diverse styles of Chenin Blanc being produced around the world.

One can't completely appreciate (or even discuss) Chenin Blanc without taking into account what the South Africans have done with it over the past 400 or so years. That's why I located Jim Clarke, the US Marketing Manager for WOSA.

"Chenin Blanc was one of the first varietals brought to South Africa by the Dutch in 1655," he told me. "It's the most planted wine grape in the country." According to Mr. Clarke, South Africa has more plantings of Chenin Blanc than any other wine-producing region – in fact, more than the rest of the world combined.

Why, then, are so few people familiar with it?

Part of the reason, of course, was the country's unfortunate political history. International trade sanctions because of apartheid prevented the country's products (including wine) from being exported. And for many years, the entire wine industry was under the firm control of a government agency that pretty much quashed experimentation, and barred new varietals from entering the country. That's all changed.

"South Africa has a wide variety of micro-climates," notes Jim Clarke. "That means it can be made in many different styles. In France, Chenin Blanc is a cool climate variety. In South Africa, the climate is warmer. The acidity is lower, but the flavors are still balanced on the palate."

The major regions you'll see on Chenin Blanc labels from South Africa include Paarl, Swartland, and Breedkloof, though other regions produce the wine as well. Most of it is exported to the UK, Germany, and Holland, but more is finding its way to our shores. Even though many prominent South African sports celebrities (mostly golfers like Ernie Els) have gone into the wine business in the country, they have mostly concentrated on the so-called "international" varietals, like Cabernet Sauvignon and Syrah. But South African Chenin Blanc sales in the U.S. continue to climb every year.

To boost their wine trade even further, WOSA sponsors a protégé program that helps disadvantaged groups train for and secure jobs in the industry. The De Bos winery offers their employees ownership positions. "At DeBos, over 25% of the employees are part owners," says Clarke.

Admittedly, this is not a wine you lay down in the cellar for 20 years. But if you like Pinot Grigio and similar light and food-friendly wines, Chenin Blanc is a good choice. Plus, it's made in a variety of styles, so if you sample widely (always a good idea) you're sure to find a few you'll enjoy.

Rosé Revisited

Every once in a while, it's a good idea to take another look at a wine or a grape varietal that we've discussed in the past. Even though I've written about it earlier in this book, sometimes wines go out of fashion and then come back. They do that. Other times new types or styles of a particular wine are developed and find their way to the market. And then there's the seasonal situation: we generally write about and review wines that are suitable for the weather and time of year.

Personally, I've never quite believed that we HAVE to drink ONLY whites in the summer, and ONLY full-bodied reds during cooler seasons. But, having sampled widely and with great dedication, I've arrived at a conclusion about rosé. It's this: these wines are excellent choices pretty much whenever.

As I've mentioned in the past, you can make rosé wines in two different ways. It's perfectly legitimate to simply mix some red and white together, which is how many of them are created. Or, if you do it the classier and more expensive way, you crush red grapes, leave the juice on the skins until the liquid achieves the color you want, then drain it off.

Plus, rosés can be made from just about any red varietal. In Tavel in southern France, many are made from Grenache and Syrah, which are the major grapes in the region, but we've sampled others made from Zinfandel and even Pinot Noir.

Since these wines come in such a wide variety of styles, you're sure to find one that's light enough or full-bodied enough, or dry or sweet enough to accompany almost any kind of food and any type of occasion. And, since excellent rosés are made all over the world, you can choose the traditional styles from the south of France (especially Tavel and Lirac) or other types from California, Washington State, or even South America.

Riesling Reconsidered

I have a confession to make. As widely as I sample and write about wine, there has always been something of a vacant space in my wine appreciation, and it's the wines of Germany. Our collection is packed with bottles from California, Washington State, France, Italy, and some stranger places like Moldova. But I've never been able to get my arms around the way German wine producers classify and label their products.

Until now.

On a trip to Germany, I set out to get myself educated about Riesling, which is the predominant varietal in the region, as well as some of the lesser-known wines, like Gruner Veltliner, Müller-Thurgau, and Gewürztraminer. Glad I did.

The problem has been that the Germans classify their wines – and label them – in a very unconventional way: by level of sweetness. Second, a producer might make fifteen or twenty different wines from various blocks in the vineyard. And third, until recently, German wine labels were gorgeously colorful works of art with completely unreadable Gothic lettering. Add to that descriptive terminology like "Trocken-beerenauslese" and "Qualitatswein mit Pradikat," and American consumers (like me) can perhaps be excused for scratching their heads in puzzlement. And, like many people, I originally believed that most, if not all, Rieslings were very sweet.

But here's what I discovered. Not only are Rieslings at all levels of sweetness great food wines, but the winemakers have started labeling their bottles in a much more contemporary – and readable – style.

Our visit to the village of Bernkastel on the Mosel River was a revelation. We were hosted at a private tasting by Bart Kroth, whose family has been making wine in the area for about 500 years, though he doesn't look that old. Bart guided us through several styles of Rieslings that he creates from some of the world's steepest vineyards.

Many of his samples were quite dry, acidic, and complex, but, of course, there were some sweeter styles, which are designated *Auslese, Beerenauslese,* and *Trockenbeerenauslese,* in order of increasing sugar content.

Characteristic flavors of this varietal include peach, honey, citrus, and apricot. In a way, it's the opposite of Chardonnay. It's grown with great success not only in Germany, where it's indigenous, but in Alsace, Washington State, Australia, the Finger Lakes of New York, and even South America.

Now for the bad news and good news. Many of the best examples of Riesling from Germany are imported in very small quantities, often less than 100-200 cases, and they can be pricey. The good news: Rieslings from the US and other parts of the world are plentiful, respectably rated, and reasonably priced.

Sauvignon Blanc - The Bottle That Did it For Me

Maybe some of the Kiwis from the South Island would argue with this, but to my mind, the New Zealanders have taken the art of making Sauvignon Blanc completely over the top. Now, it's true that many of the SBs from that part of the world are a bit predictable and similar in their flavor profile, but there's still plenty of variety in the various producers and regions.

Let's go back a bit. I've written in the past that people who become passionate about wine (maybe not to the point where they become wine writers and educators, but...) have had an epiphany somewhere along the way. Someone pours you a glass of something, you taste it, and say, "Holy moley, I never knew anything could taste like that." You are transformed...and pretty much lost forever.

For wife Debi and me, it was a glass of Cloudy Bay Sauvignon Blanc from Marlborough, New Zealand, back in 1995. Life changing, and I'm serious about that. However, when I looked back over my previous columns, I was shocked – shocked – to discover that I had never written about this particular varietal. Let's correct that omission right now.

First, the Sauvignon Blanc grape is pretty much native to the Loire Valley in France, and grown at the eastern end of the river, primarily around the villages of Pouilly and Sancerre. It's made in many styles. Visit one winery, and all the wine is resting in oak barrels. Go to the winery across the street, and there's not a stick of wood anywhere; everything is stainless steel.

Typically, characteristics of this refreshing white wine include grapefruit, pineapple, hay, maybe some lychee and gooseberry, and often a whiff of what we politely call *pipi du chat*. As strange as that may sound, the slight aroma of what Scruffy does in the litterbox is very much part of the flavor profile of many Sauvignon Blancs. To be a bit less coarse about it, most critics refer to that particular aroma as "boxwood." Strangely enough, it works.

Nevertheless. This is a wine that pairs incredibly well with a wide range of dishes, especially if they involve seafood. I have formulated what I call the "lemon law." If you can put lemon ON it, you can drink Sauvignon Blanc WITH it. This is especially true of shellfish, and even more so with Florida's famous stone crabs, available only during months with an "R" in them. If you want a treat, just buy a few pounds of claws and wash them down with a bottle of New Zealand's finest. The flavors of the New Zealand wines are very much up front. Some would say they're more "obvious." The flavors of grapefruit, pineapple, and citrus mentioned above are unmistakable, and hit you as soon as you put your nose in the glass. Not necessarily a bad thing.

My favorite New Zealand producers are Cloudy Bay (of course), Villa Maria, Nobilo, Oyster Bay, and Kim

Crawford. The Cloudy Bay runs around $35 a bottle, but the other brands are more economical.

Do You Know the Way to Viognier?

Yes, it's pronounced vee-own-YAY, but that's because it's French, like most of the major wine grapes of the world...and it's a white wine you should really get to know.

Its spiritual home is the northern Rhône Valley, and specifically the tiny appellation of Condrieu. And tiny it is. Condrieu is less than 400 acres, and includes the miniscule sub-appellation of Chateau-Grillet, which grows less than nine acres of this very interesting white grape. Problem is, that this is a naturally low-yielding varietal, so vineyards don't produce tons of it, and many winemakers don't find it profitable to bother with.

But there's good news. In the rest of the world, like North and South America, New Zealand and even Israel, many talented winemakers are supporting and promoting Viognier wines, and with good reason. There are significant plantings in California and Australia, and winemakers in Virginia have also taken up the challenge. Plus, I've had some excellent examples of this varietal while traveling in Uruguay.

California has a group of ambitious winemakers called the Rhône Rangers, who devote themselves to cultivating the traditional grapes of that region, such as Grenache, Syrah, Mourvedre, and others. Since the mid-1980s they've done quite a bit to promote Viognier cultivation and popularize the wine.

Sidebar – In Australia, many Syrah producers blend about 5% of Viognier into their reds, where it amplifies the aromas and bouquet of the wine.

But enough of that. What does it taste like? The real charm of Viognier is its very pronounced and characteristic floral aromas. Many people find that it offers a drinking experience similar to Chardonnay. The difference is that while Chardonnay gets many of its aromatic components from oak aging and malolactic fermentation, Viognier has a whole set of natural aromas that are quite distinctive – and extremely pleasant. When you taste it for the first time, you will recognize it instantly every time afterward. There are flower and fruit aromas that are also found in sweeter wines like Muscat and Riesling, but Viognier is generally produced in a refreshing dry style, and is meant to be enjoyed young.

Back to those aromas. You'll generally sense pronounced notes of peach, white flowers like honeysuckle and jasmine, tangerine, and often a hint of vanilla. Lovely.

The floral aromas and fruit flavors put it in the same category as acidic German varietals like Gewürztraminer, and make it an excellent accompaniment to spicy cuisines, like Thai and Indian. It also complements shellfish, veal, and pork.

So here's the bottom line. If you're a big Chardonnay fan (and who isn't?) this wine is a refreshing change of pace.

The Other Cabernet

As we all know, Cabernet Sauvignon is one of the world's most favorite and most celebrated wines. It's one of the six "noble varietals," so called because it's capable of making elegant wines that can age and develop for decades. It reaches its ultimate expression, according to many, as a major component of the Bordeaux blend, and in many of the highest quality wines from California – especially from Napa Valley.

But hold on a second. There's another Cabernet called Cabernet Franc…and it's worth knowing about – and enjoying. It's one of the world's major black grapes, kind of a twin cousin to Sauvignon, and also makes big, dark, bold reds that pair beautifully with many types of foods…especially those with a higher salt content (think Asian flank steak and other dishes with soy sauce). And it's also a component, along with Merlot and Petit Verdot, of the traditional blend of the finest wines from France's Bordeaux region.

The heart of traditional the traditional Cab Franc growing region is just at the middle of the Loire Valley, around the villages of Chinon and Bourgueil, which is, as everyone knows, pronounced "burr-GOOEY." It's southwest of Tours, and not remotely near any other major city. But the countryside is gorgeous…and so is the food. Of course, it's grown extensively in Bordeaux, and popular in other winegrowing regions such as Italy, Hungary, and the USA. Interestingly, the Canadians have taken a fancy to it, growing it around Niagara on the Lake, and in the Okanagan Valley in British Columbia, where they use it to make ice wine.

Cabernet Franc, as mentioned, is closely related to Cabernet Sauvignon, but it's not as dark, and has a softer level of intensity. The perfume is a bit richer, with aromas of raspberries, tobacco, cassis, and violets. The tannins are more rounded as well, so it tends to have a smoother mouthfeel. A wine like Justin "Justification" is a good example, coming from Paso Robles and containing a healthy percentage of Merlot for a softer mouthfeel and rounder tannins.

 The truth is that this grape is used in blends probably more than it's bottled as a single varietal. However, there's a lot of enjoyment to be had. So look for it the next time you go wine shopping.

PART II
THE GROUND

*T*he roots of the vines go down, way down, sucking up the minerals and flavors of the soil. Then add in the culture and history of the region and the fact that they don't make wine in ugly places. Drink it, and you'll want to go there.

Soon after my wife and I fell into the delights of wine appreciation, we were compelled to travel to where it's made. And a well-known wine writer whom I greatly respect once said that there is something very special about drinking wine in the place where it comes from. During a trip to the Loire Valley some years ago, I confirmed that he was right.

This section is a tribute to the many (but not all) places in the world that are fortunate enough to have the right climate, soil, geography, and culture to grow wine grapes successfully and convert them into the beverage we all enjoy.

Kiwis, Hobbits, Glaciers, and Lots of Sheep

While I've written in the past about Sauvignon Blanc from California, Chile and other excellent regions, there are two places in the world where this particular wine really finds a home. The first, of course, is the Loire Valley in France, where the grape is believed to have originated, and where it reaches a truly pure expression. The second is New Zealand, where it's crafted in a completely different style. Of course, we have to sample them both, but we'll deal with the Loire another time.

When wine geeks discuss the subject among themselves, one question is often asked: "What was the bottle that did it for you?" Meaning, what wine did you taste that opened your eyes, triggered the passion, changed your life and wounded your wallet? For us, it was a New Zealand Sauvignon Blanc. Cloudy Bay, in fact, which, at the time, back around 1995, did much to put New Zealand wines on the worldwide map.

Unlike the relatively subtle Sauvignon Blancs from the Loire, the Kiwis are a whole different barrel of juice. Their wines smack you in the face with fresh zingy flavors of grapefruit, pineapple, gooseberry, lychee, and grass on a firm frame of bright acidity. It's a fundamental truth that wine is a product of the culture that creates it, and reflects that culture. This stuff sort of proves the point. It expresses the New Zealanders themselves...friendly, open, hospitable, and easy to like. Best of all, some excellent examples (90-92 points) can be had in the $20 and under range.

As you probably know, the country is comprised of the North Island and the South Island, and wine is made from one end to the other. While the Marlborough region at the top of the South Island is probably best known, don't hesitate to sample the offerings from places like Gisbourne, Martinborough, and Hawke's Bay. And, even though they don't often make it to the US, wines from Waiheke Island, just off the coast near Auckland, are a lot of fun if you can find them.

Another thing we love about New Zealand is that you can visit Hobbiton, and steep yourself in the whole Lord of the Rings experience. When we were there, the village had just been completely renovated for the filming of the prequel. If you're a fan, this is not to be missed.

On the South Island, as mentioned, there are two major regions: Marlborough and Central Otago, which is at the very south end, not far from the Southern Alps. The former is known primarily for Sauvignon

Blanc and some Chardonnay, while Central Otago has made a major mark in recent years by producing some excellent Pinot Noir at insanely reasonable prices.

Running Down the Rhône

When writing about the wines of France's Rhône valley, the hardest thing is remembering to put that little *accent circumflex* over the "o" all the time. It's a pain. But the rest of it is pure pleasure, because the wines of this region offer tremendous taste treats, and tremendous values.

First things first. The area is divided into two parts, Northern and Southern, which have absolutely nothing to do with each other. They're separated by about 40 miles of agricultural land with nary a grapevine to be seen, and their winemaking traditions are worlds apart. In the North, the predominant red grape is Syrah, but in the south, the reds are blends of Syrah, Grenache, Mourvedre, and up to ten other grapes. In both areas, whites, which represent only a small part of the production, are generally Viognier, Roussanne, and Marsanne. More about those whites another time.

The northernmost area of the Northern Rhône is called the Côte Rôtie...the "roasted slope." Just to the south is the famous area of Hermitage, with its landmark hill rising above a bend in the river. The southern Rhône is best known for Châteauneuf du Pape, and that's a column (or an entire book) in itself.

In the most general sense, the north, which starts near the town of Vienne, includes (from north to south) the appellations of Condrieu (100% whites), St. Joseph (very popular), Cornas, and the famous area of Hermitage. As mentioned above, production is almost all red wines, and they're made with 100% Syrah.

Here's another little wrinkle: the Côte Rôtie itself consists of two parts...the Côte Brune and the Côte Blonde. These are separate hillsides, and wines may come from either one, or can be a blend from both areas. In fact, Guigal, a major producer, has a wine called "Brune et Blonde," which is very well known. The hillsides are so named because the Blonde has lighter colored soils, and the Brune is darker.

And one more item, if I may: even though the red wine of the northern Rhone is Syrah, they often like to blend in just a little Viognier (a white wine). Not much, maybe about 5% or so, more for aroma than anything else. The Aussies do the same thing.

In this region, they do things a little differently, using some practices that are absolutely against the law in other places. Specifically, they use a technique called *chaptalization*, charmingly named after Jean-Antoine Chaptal, the Minister of Agriculture under Napoleon. This practice involves adding sugar to the fermenting juice to boost the alcohol content. Most places in the world, it's illegal.

There are hundreds of producers in this area, and they've been in the winemaking game for a very long time. Many are *negociants*, which means they buy grapes from various growers, make and blend their own wines, and bottle them under their own labels. This is not necessarily a bad thing, and you might look for wines from Guigal, Paul Jaboulet Aine, and

Chapoutier. (Chapoutier, by the way, prints his wine labels in Braille).

As I've mentioned many times, the wine world is a very big place. It's probably easier to start with the northern area, since there's only one red varietal to worry about, then work your way south, ending with the very complex (and complicated) wines of Châteauneuf du Pape.

The "Other" Aussies

The wine world knows all about the Australians. Big bold reds...zingy whites. But what about the other Aussies...the Austrians? Even though they're also making bold reds and zingy whites, this country's wines haven't resonated with American consumers as much as they deserve to. That needs to change.

Problem is, the Austrians faced extreme hardship in the mid 1980s when several wineries were discovered diluting their wines with ethylene glycol, which you and I know as antifreeze, and we also know it's poisonous. The scandal virtually destroyed the country's wine industry, but good things come from bad. Stringent new laws were passed -- and enforced -- so Austrian wines are not only better than they used to be, they're well up to international quality.

It's also a bit confusing to American consumers that Austrian wines are labeled with much the same system used in Germany. They're classified by sweetness, then by the region of origin, and then by quality, from ordinary table wine to the higher end versions. So if you see a label that reads "Velich

Welschriesling Trockenbeerenauslese Neusiedlersee,"
nobody would blame you if you stood there scratching
your head.

Today, however, the Austrians have climbed aboard
the international bandwagon in a big way. They've
simplified the labeling, put the name of the grape on
the bottle, and directed their efforts to creating more
commercial – and more fulfilling – reds and whites
with traditional flavor profiles.

The major winegrowing regions are all located in the
agricultural eastern part of the country. The premiere
areas are Wachau, along with Burgenland and Styria,
all of which are divided into several subregions.

As mentioned before, the wines are classified in a
manner a bit strange to us in the New World, so look
for the "Qualitätswein" designation. Not surprisingly,
it means "quality wine," and it will come from a single
district. The bottle top will have a red and white seal.
One level up from that is "Kabinett," which is
Qualitätswein and then some.

About those grapes: they're not your typical
international varietals with names we all know and
love. Even though the Austrians are becoming
internationally minded in their marketing and
labeling, the grapes they grow are very much their
own. And that's a good thing.

For white wines, aside from the sweet ones, Grüner
Veltliner is well worth a try. It's generally dry, with
tropical fruit overtones, and we enjoy it with Indian
food, Thai, and similar dishes that are hard to match
with conventional wines. Of course, they grow

Riesling, and another white grape known as Müller-Thurgau (don't forget the umlaut...), though you're not likely to see it bottled as a single varietal.

The reds are big. While they do grow international varietals like Pinot Noir, the real interest is in the native grapes like Blaufränkisch, Zweigelt, and St. Laurent. For me, the St. Laurent grape is capable of producing wines of true elegance and power. However, about half the red wine produced in Austria comes from the Zweigelt grape, and that's not a bad thing.

Zweigelt is an easy-drinking wine, not too tannic, that usually displays cherry and cassis flavors, much like a Cabernet, only lighter. Blaufränkisch is more structured, more powerful, and capable of aging. The cherry and cassis notes are there, but you'll get more complexity, and more levels of flavor, including blackberry, earth, and spice.

Sidebar...Austria is also the home of the Riedel family who, as all wine lovers know, makes probably the finest wine glasses in the world. They come in a staggering array of shapes and sizes for all kinds of wine. The family stays in business not only because of the quality of their glassware, but also because of the fragility. Riedel glasses will explode into glittering crystal shards if you so much as look at them the wrong way. So then you buy new ones.

Way Up West?

They sure do like to make wine along the west coast of the US. The styles and varietals run from high quality Cabernets (California) to gorgeous Pinot Noirs (Oregon) to big, bold Syrahs (Washington). And the region extends up to British Columbia, as well. Actually, the whole Pacific Northwest area has been growing grapes for a long time, but they used to make juice and jelly out of them. It's been only since the mid-1970s that they've become serious about fine wine. The last 30 years have been a boom.

Basically, the general weather pattern is the same as in Burgundy, a fact that Pinot Noir growers absolutely adore. However, the warm Pacific current that brings the rains is extremely variable, so vintages are a bit more important in that area.

Winegrowing regions vary widely in a number of respects. Of course, there's the climate, the soil, the latitude, all that. Then there's the ease (or lack of it) with which intrepid tourists can make their way to the different wineries and tasting rooms. Some areas are set up for it and others...not so much.

Napa Valley is. Just get on Route 29 in the city of Napa and make your way north. The wineries are as close together as McMansions on the beach, and you can hit a whole bunch of them each day. Sonoma is a different story. It's more rural, and you need to drive a bit more, so it's important to be judicious in your consumption.

Oregon is, for the most part. In the Willamette area, many wineries are on a main road, and weaving from one to the other isn't all that tough. Just like in Napa or Sonoma, you can drive along a few central roads, hitting one vineyard tasting room after another. However, Washington is set up differently. The eastern part of the state is desert, which is perfect for growing thick-skinned red grapes, like Cabernet, Syrah, and some Spanish varietals. In fact, the state is second in wine production after California. The bad news is that wine country is on the other side of the Cascade Mountains, and a tough trip from the population centers in the west. Result: almost all wineries have tasting rooms in the major cities, like Seattle, and aren't all that set up for tourists at the winery. Too bad, because part of wine appreciation is drinking it where it's made, and tasting rooms in some downtown area, no matter how nicely decorated, just don't have the charm.

The folks in Washington don't stop at reds. Weather conditions force the grapes to ripen early, if they ripen at all, so growers have had a lot of luck with zippy, acidic wines, like Sauvignon Blanc. And, since the climate is a bit like the Alsace region between France and Germany, you'll find some great Rieslings from the area. The semi-ripening of those white grapes yields wines that are lean and acidic, with lower alcohol. Chateau Ste. Michelle's "Eroica" Riesling is very popular, in a semi-sweet style.

The Columbia Valley, and the several vineyard regions around it (Walla Walla, Horse Heaven Hills, Rattlesnake Hills, etc.) get about 8 inches of rain a year, which makes irrigation absolutely vital. There's lots of sun in the summer, and early onset of cold weather. It's a terrible place to grow anything but apples and wine grapes. Plus, the area is vast. The Columbia Valley appellation alone covers almost half the state, and some of it spills over into Oregon. So there are hotels and restaurants, a wine tourism industry, and almost 700 registered wineries, but it's a heck of a ride to get out there.

It's certainly worth the trip to eastern Washington, and the state's wines are definitely worth a trip to the supermarket or your favorite store. First of all, in addition to some nice Chardonnays and elegant Rieslings, the area's long suit is big, mouthwatering reds. They grow over 80 types of grapes up there, but you should look mainly for Cabernet Sauvignon, Syrah, and (if you can find them) wines made from Cabernet Franc and even Nebbiolo, which is the primary grape in the big expensive Barolos from northern Italy.

Sicily: The Wines You Can't Refuse

Since practically the beginning of time, the Romans (then the Italians) have been toying with the idea of building a bridge over the Straits of Messina to link the island of Sicily with the mainland. Hasn't happened yet. Maybe never will.

This makes a visit to Sicily a bit of a hike, but one that's well worth taking, especially since there are direct flights from Rome to three of the island's major cities. The scenery is incredible -- there are more Greek temples in Sicily than in Greece itself -- and the wines are spectacular – especially the varietals you never heard of.

For practically ever, Sicilian grapes were used for raisins, while certain varietals were grown to make Marsala, a sweet wine that most people associate with Sicily, if they think about it at all. But over the last 30 years or so, the Sicilians have realized that they can make great wine...and they've become very hip to international grape varietals. In fact, Sicily is one of the two largest wine producing areas in Italy, which is saying quite a bit. Producers such as Planeta, Regaleali and Donnafugata make Chardonnays, Syrahs, and other wines that hold their own against anything that comes from the mainland. But if you really want to pick up some great bargains, look for the wines made from grapes that are indigenous to the island.

Sicily is located, after all, in the Mediterranean, and the coastline is studded with palm trees, so the balmy climate isn't suited to growing zippy, acidic wines. The Chardonnays tend to be big, bold, and buttery, with deep flavors – not the lean, minerally Burgundian style at all. And since the warm weather causes the grapes to get extremely ripe, the reds are deep, dark, brooding...and intensely alcoholic.

Aside from the Chardonnays, I personally find Sicilian whites to be undistinguished. A possible exception: the Bianco d'Alcamo, grown in Trapani on the extreme western end of the island. It's made from a grape called Catarratto, with a few other whites thrown in. It's dry and fruity and fun, but by no means a major wine.

The big fun is in the reds. Our two favorites are Nerello Mascalese and Nero d'Avola, both of them deep, dark, and great with food.

Nero d'Avola, as the name indicates, is native to Avola in the extreme southeast corner of the island, near Siracusa. However, the grape is now grown everywhere, and just about every Sicilian producer makes it. The good news is, no matter which kind you buy, it's probably going to be good. Since I sample so widely (ahem...) I've tasted Neros from many of the major producers, and never met one I didn't like. The wine has an intense ruby color and flavors of dark fruit, earth, and aromatic herbs. It's a big, satisfying wine, and great with grilled meats. The two major producers are Regaleali and Duca di Salaparuta, but don't let that deter you from trying others.

At the eastern end of the island, the still-active volcano of Mt. Etna broods over the landscape. It's 10,000 feet high, snow-capped all year round, and emits a steady column of white steam into the deep blue sky, just to let us know it's not dead yet. But on the eastern slope the Nerello Mascalese grapes grow, and while we might never think to walk into a wine store and ask for a bottle, maybe we should.

Often blended with other wines, Nerello Mascalese makes a great quaff in its pure form. Medium bodied, spicy, and with strong notes of deep fruit, violets, earth, and forest floor, it's a bit like Cabernet Sauvignon, and pairs well with steaks, chops, and other hearty meats.

So be curious...adventurous, and take a chance on a Sicilian wine the next time you browse the aisles of your favorite store. It's worth the trip.

Heresy, Popes, and Wine

Once upon a time, a friend conned me into splitting a case of red from the Languedoc. It turned out to be clean, tasty, and inexpensive, so I hauled out my

trusty wine atlas and asked some Serious Questions.
Where *is* the Languedoc, anyway? What's the
weather like? Do they have any good Mexican
restaurants?

As it turns out, the Languedoc is in the south of
France (I actually guessed France right away),
running roughly parallel to the Mediterranean coast.
There are pitifully few enchilada establishments, but
the inhabitants compensate by growing sensational
grapes and making wonderful wine which they insist
on selling at comically low prices. They all live in tiny
villages with names like *Nissan-les-Enserune*, which
means "Your Japanese car has leaked brake fluid on
my new Reeboks," and *Aspiran,* which means either
"heavy breathing" or "headache relief," depending on
the local dialect.

The big discovery: sometimes wine is the way it is not
just because of the grapes, or the ground, or the guy
or gal who made it, but because of long-ago
historical events and imperatives.

The Languedoc is a perfect example, thanks to the
Albigensian Crusade, which was so named because
it was centered around the town of Albi, the
birthplace of Toulouse-Latrec, though he was not
home at the time. The Albigensian Crusade was a
wave of religious persecution, a common pastime
back then (and still today), and it had a direct effect
on what was in the case of wine I was forced to buy.

Lotario di Segni was elected Pope in 1198, and took
the name Innocent III, which just shows what a
puckish sense of humor he had, because innocence
was far from his most distinguishing character trait.

He immediately set about convincing everyone in Western Europe that the Pope was superior in power and authority to any earthly or lay ruler. This, unsurprisingly, did little to endear him to the kings and princes of Europe's many city-states, most of whom Di Segni excommunicated on a depressingly regular basis. He threw the Count of Toulouse out of the church *twelve times.*

During that era a bunch of Christians around the town of Albi decided that traditional Catholicism wasn't exactly blowing their collective skirts up, and adopted some pretty weird beliefs that were far outside of Catholic orthodoxy. The beliefs of the Cathari, as they were known, spread fairly rapidly because they preached incessantly until people converted just to make them go away, and they quickly rose to positions of influence. Remains of their castles can still be seen in the Languedoc.

Anyway, Innocent III finally got fed up with the fact that there were people running around the south of France believing in weird unorthodox stuff. To get them to mend their ways, he sent St. Bernard of Clairvaux, wandering friars, papal legates, everybody but the Vienna Boys' Choir, to preach around Albi and gently show the Cathari the error of their ways. Didn't help.

Finally, Innocent declared the Albigensian Crusade, which sent throngs of knights and soldiers into the area to root out the heresy once and for all. Not surprisingly, the crusaders quickly directed their efforts toward political and economic, rather than spiritual, ends, and spent their days doing what most invading armies of the time did -- looting and burning.

When the unfortunate winemaking villagers in the Languedoc didn't give the Crusaders the Right Answer when questioned about their beliefs, the invaders would kill every living thing in sight and then *burn the vineyards*. That's why the wines of this region are so good: because of the burning. Over time, as the vineyards were restored, new and exciting grape varieties sprouted up. Today, the area grows mainly Carignan, Cinsault, Grenache, Syrah, and Mourvèdre. There is also a healthy amount of Chardonnay. The wines of this region are spectacular bargains.

South Africa On the Move

There are 54 countries in Africa, but only eight of them produce wine. As you might expect, South Africa leads the pack, and it's the 7th largest wine producer in the world. Recently, the wine industry in that country has been more assertive in promoting their wines, and that's not a bad thing. Several of the varietals we've sampled recently definitely deserve a place in the cellar...and on the table.

The first wines in the country were made over 300 years ago by Dutch colonists, but it wasn't until the 1990s that South Africa really began to take its place in the wine world. As discussed in the section on Chenin Blanc, international trade sanctions were imposed because of apartheid. And secondly, the entire industry was controlled by a government agency called KWV, which severely limited the kinds of grapes that could be grown. Plus, the culture was more oriented toward beer, and the country is one of the world's top beer markets. I'm told that beer costs less than Coca Cola over there.

In South Africa, the workhorse grape has traditionally been Pinotage. Unfortunately, it's a hybrid that's not really capable of making the quality of wine that can compete in the international marketplace. Thankfully, in the past 10-15 years, they've turned toward the more classic varietals, and today there are some high-quality bargains to be had.

The major wine regions are around Capetown, because the climate is similar to the warmer areas along the Mediterranean. The names you'll see on the label include Constantia, Franschhoek, Paarl, and Stellenbosch, which has a university that includes a viticultural department. So they're getting serious.

As mentioned in the last section, most of the wines from South Africa have been white. Their Chenin Blanc, which they call Steen, is generally world class, followed closely by Chardonnay, Riesling, and Sauvignon Blanc. They're also getting good at sparkling whites, some made in the traditional Champagne method, others made more like Prosecco or Spanish Cava.

The reds, which include Shiraz and Cabernet, are almost all aged in American oak, which gives them a particular richness. You can expect flavors of cherry, plum, and coffee...and a pleasant smokiness which is the result of a (harmless) virus that has affected South African grapes for decades.

So the next time you're browsing in the wine aisle, give South African wines a bit of consideration. These days, they deserve it.

Israeli Wine is Real Wine

Wine lovers love to share. If we discover a new wine or producer or region, we can't wait to pour a glass for our friends. My wife Debi and I make a lot of our discoveries an annual blast called the Wine Experience.

At the end of every October, we journey to the annual New York Wine Experience, staged by *Wine Spectator* magazine. It's a three-day festival of grand tastings and conducted food and wine seminars, and it's always full of surprises. The grand tastings on Thursday and Friday evenings feature over 260 wineries offering generous samples of their top-rated wines. Incidentally, all the wines at the event received 90 points or higher from the *Wine Spectator* tasting panel. So every glass is right up there, in terms of quality.

The wines come from all over the world, and at the 2016 Wine Experience I was delightfully surprised to find not one, but four Israeli wines included in the event. This was a first.

It's no surprise that most people think of kosher wine as sweet and sticky, like Manishewitz or Mogen David. But that was then. Today, young, talented winemakers are cultivating the ancient soils and turning out world class wines (some kosher, some not) from international varietals like Cabernet Sauvignon,

Merlot, and Chardonnay. Many of the producers received their winemaking education at world-class schools like UC Davis and other very respectable institutions.

Frankly, I didn't know what to expect as I made my way through the crush of people in the Marriott Marquis ballroom. But I did know that Israeli wines had caught the attention of the folks at *Wine Spectator* because they'd actually done a cover story on the subject in the issue that came out a week before the Wine Experience. "Surprising Quality From an Emerging Region," said the cover. Right on.

While kosher wines have had a somewhat dubious reputation in the US in the past, those days are long gone. The fact that a wine is kosher makes no difference in the flavor profile. In fact, not all Israeli wines are kosher. Today's wines – especially the ones we sampled in New York -- stand up to anything currently coming out of France, California, or anywhere.

Besides, when you stop to think about it, the region practically invented wine. And when you visit the Holy Land to see the places that are sacred to your religion, what could be better than combining your pilgrimage with a wine tour?

Admittedly, the selection of Israeli wines at your local store may be a bit underwhelming, but many are available online. Check wine-searcher.com.

So...Israel offers younger winemakers who have solid schooling and experience, international varietals made in international styles, and the advantage of soils in the Golan Heights and Judean Hills that have been hallowed by thousands of years of wine production. If the wine is good, it can come from anywhere.

G'Day...It's Australian Wine Time

We're at lunch in McLaren Vale, sitting across from Sparky and Sarah Marquis, with several glasses of their legendary Carnival of Love Shiraz in front of us. As I sip through the vintages, I'm blown away because their wines are consistently ranked in the world's Top 100, and because the wine is arguably one of the purest expressions of what Australian winemaking is all about.

Americans like the Aussie approach so much that the country will soon be the second largest importer of wine to the US. For a country that spent much of its winegrowing history making sweet wines (which they call "stickies"), that's quite an achievement.

In this category, it's the big fruity reds that most vividly capture our attention and interest. In fact, the big Shirazes and blends can be so powerful they need to age for eons before you'd dare open the bottle. (I attended a vertical tasting of Penfold's Grange a few years ago, and we drank the 1971. It could have used another 10 years in the cellar).

Unlike other countries, most Aussie wines, even the greatest ones, are blended from fruit that's sourced from very extensive areas. The designated winegrowing regions are enormous, and the grapes that wind up in the bottle may come from hundreds of miles in every direction. It would be like Napa winemakers blending in grapes from as far away as Washington State. They'd sooner slit their wrists.

Another thing that makes Australian wines so much fun is that they like to put puckish and whimsical names on their bottles. The Monkey Spider. The Dead Arm. The Stump Jump. Woop Woop.

Considering their winemaking success, the Australians have no native grapes. Everything grown in the country originated at one time or another from cuttings brought from Europe and South Africa in the late 18th and early 19th centuries.

Until next time....g'day, mate! (They really do say that.)

Discover the "Other" California

There's no question that the Golden State is the center of America's winemaking industry. Of course, we're more than receptive to the wines from Washington State and Oregon. Fact is, one of my favorite Champagne-style wines is made in Albuquerque, New Mexico, and I still haven't figured that one out.

But still...when we think of California wines, we naturally turn first to Napa Valley, and then, after a moment, to Sonoma. There are fabulous wines made in both those places, and many of them have become hysterically expensive.

That's why it's fun to go beyond the familiar names and places, searching for values from a bit farther off the well-beaten track. Since the areas aren't quite so famous, the wines are more in our ballpark, pricewise. Here are three places to look.

The Sierra Foothills -- The main area of this winegrowing region is Amador County, the center of the old Gold Rush days. Many of those aspiring gold miners were German and Italian, and wine is what they drank. As mentioned in the section on Zinfandel, hundreds of acres of Zinfandel vines in the area are well over 60 years old. Older vines produce richer wines, which is why you'll often see the words "old vines" or "ancient vines" on the label.

Lake County – This area is just up the road from Napa, with the winegrowing area centered, not surprisingly, around Clear Lake, which is the largest natural lake in the state. There are four districts, each with a different soil type, so there's a wide variety of flavor profiles to choose from.

Lodi – If you draw a line directly south from Sacramento, and another one directly east from San Francisco, Lodi is where they cross. It happens to be the original home of the Mondavi family, who settled here before moving up to the Napa area. Lodi specializes in Zinfandel, with Cabernet Sauvignon running a close second.

So. If you can bring yourself to take a chance on a California winegrowing district that may not be all that familiar, wonderful discoveries await.

Taking the Oregon Challenge

Oregon is a tough place to grow grapes. There's not much sun or heat, but plenty of rain, and frost. Fortunately, Pinot Noir grapes love that kind of weather. We discussed this a bit in the section on

West Coast wines, but the topic deserves a bit more detailed attention.

The popularity of Oregon Pinot Noir actually started back in 1979. At an international exposition in France, over 600 Pinot Noirs were tasted and judged blind. As mentioned in Part I, a wine from Oregon's Eyrie Vineyards came in third. "Sacre bleu," said the French. How is it possible that a wine from (gasp) *America* can make the grade against the legendary (and incredibly expensive) Pinot Noirs from Burgundy? Something's wrong. We want a rematch.

You'll remember that they had another blind tasting in 1980. Eyrie came in second. In a big hurry, some of the most prestigious Burgundian wine producers flocked to Oregon, bought land, planted grapes, and they're just as happy as can be with how their wines are turning out.

There is probably no other grape that offers the pure romance, the sexy silkiness, of a fine Pinot Noir. The American varieties (primarily from Oregon and the Sonoma Coast region of California) are "fruit forward," offering aromas and flavors of strawberry, blackberry, and plum. The great Burgundies are driven by what the French call "terroir:" the flavors of the earth from which they come. You can expect scents of forest floor, wet leaves, spices, and herbs.

Even though some of the wines of the fabled Domaine de la Romanée-Conti in Burgundy cost around $2,000 a bottle on release, there are bargains to be found, and some sensational wines are on the shelf for under $50.

To Tuscany...And Beyond

Many first-time visitors to Tuscany head straight for Florence. And why not? There's the Uffizi Gallery, great food all over the place, and vineyards in every direction. Plus, it's a good place to start appreciating Italian wine.

Any American who's ever eaten a pizza knows about Chianti: it's the heart of the Tuscan wine region. And thankfully, the quality of those wines has improved enormously since the days when we used to choke the stuff down out of a bottle wrapped in straw. A bit more obscure – but well worth knowing – are the wines from the regions outside the area. Umbria. Abruzzo. So if we can tear ourselves away from the attractions of Florence and Siena, there are delights to discover.

Why not start with Montefalco? It's right next door to Tuscany, in Umbria, where the signature grape is a big, bold red called Sagrantino. Like the neighboring regions, they also grow a ton of Sangiovese, which is the main component of the Chianti wines we all know and love. But there's a twist.

See, they also make a wine called Rosso di Montefalco, which is a blend of Sangiovese, Sagrantino, and... whatever else they have sitting around. Could be Cabernet Sauvignon, Merlot, or even Syrah. That means producers are free to blend these wines in any proportion, so every Rosso you sample will taste a bit different. That's a good thing, because it means you can drink a lot of it, find the producers you like, and stick with them.

Or, you could travel in the opposite direction, to the west of Florence, and climb up to the utterly charming hill town of San Gimignano. It's just about the only place in Italy where the original tower structures still survive, and it's breathtaking.

Delightful, too, is the white wine that's most characteristic of the area: Vernaccia. Light, zippy, and slightly bitter, it's the perfect complement to seafood, shellfish, and even sushi.

Loving the Loire

The Loire Valley in France offers abundant attractions to the wine lover. Let's start with the chateaux. In days past, before the Revolution, the rich and famous from Paris retreated in the summer months to their homes along the river. Some of the cottages covered hundreds of thousands of square feet and had over 200 rooms. These days, many of them are either operated as luxury hotels or, better yet, as bed and breakfast inns at delightfully moderate prices.

Then, of course, are the wines. The Loire is the longest river in France, running northward from the eastern highlands and bending around to the west, ultimately emptying in to the Atlantic at Nantes. At the bend are two villages, Sancerre and Pouilly, and it is from here that many of the zingiest, classiest examples of Sauvignon Blanc have their origins.

While we might first associate Sauvignon Blanc with New Zealand, the grape is indigenous to the Loire, where it has been cultivated since around 400AD. Luckily, Sauvignon Blanc is one of the most food-friendly wines you can buy. I subscribe to my own personal "lemon law": if you can put lemon on it, you can drink Sauvignon Blanc with it. Perfect for broiled fish, shellfish, and similar dishes.

The Loire is a diverse area, and wines are made in a very wide range of styles. Some wineries use stainless steel tanks for fermentation, then age the wine in small oak barrels, which makes it fuller and rounder. In other wineries, there's not a stick of oak to be seen.

Generally, the Pouilly wines are fuller, while Sancerres are lighter, and easier to drink young. Since the villages are directly across the river from each other, they share the same climate, but not the same winemaking traditions. With a cool climate, the major characteristic of both areas is acidity. They are "zippy" whites, often with agreeable vegetal overtones such as hay, straw, and grass.

Sidebar: In addition to the fine wines of Pouilly and Sancerre, don't pass up the offerings from a region called Menetou-Salon. These lesser-known wines offer great values.

As we travel farther west, we come to the central region, anchored by the towns of Chinon and Bourgueil (pronounced *boor-GOOEY,* or something like that). In this area, there's hardly a white grape to be seen. It's the home of Cabernet Franc, a big, bold red that's a major component of the Bordeaux blend, but bottled here as a single varietal. If you like solid, mouthfilling reds, this is the stuff for you.

Keep going, and you'll find yourself in the areas of Samur and Anjou, the home of Chenin Blanc, another refreshing, acidic white. Though it originates in this region, the South Africans, who call it "Steen," make some excellent versions at decent prices.

Since the area is so diverse (we haven't even discussed Vouvray or Melon de Bourgogne yet) it may be worth a more extended visit in a future article. For now, however, I'd like to suggest a few producers to watch for. If you see their names on the label, chances are you're in for a treat...and a great value.

For Sauvignon Blanc, look for **_Pascal Jolivet, Alphonse Mellot,_** and **_Henri Bourgeois._** For Cabernet Franc, our favorites are **_Yannick Amirault_** (the big dog in the region), and **_Bernard Baudry._**

PART III
THE GUYS AND THE GALS

*W*inemakers are like chefs...each with a different philosophy, style, and approach. Give five winemakers the same grapes and you'll get five different wines. Part of the fascination.

As you fall down the rabbit hole into the Wonderland of Wine, several things start to happen. First, of course, is the appreciation of the beverage itself – learning to detect and enjoy the layers of flavors and aromas. Next comes the path to fine dining, new cuisines, and the pleasures of food and wine pairing. Some people choose the food and then decide what to drink with it. Others (need I mention names?) select the wine first, and then consider the bill of fare.

But the most gratifying part of the pursuit is in the people. Not only the fellow wine lovers one meets at tastings and other wine events, but the people who actually make the wine. We've been fortunate enough to meet and become friends with many of them, and we've never met a winemaker we didn't like. They are invariably interesting, dedicated people who live by ideals and philosophies that they are able to state with remarkable eloquence.

This section, then, is a compilation of interviews I've conducted with many winemakers my wife and I have come to know (and love) throughout the years.

Tor Kenward.
The Winemaker in the Candy Factory.

Normally, you don't just drop everything, run up to Napa Valley, and start making wine. And if you do, you don't always meet with success. But when the impulse, the urge, whatever you want to call it, does hit, the power can be undeniable. That's what happened to Tor Kenward, and that's what compelled him to make top-quality wines.

In his early 20s (he won't say how many years ago that was) he was a partner in a Southern California jazz club. "I fell in with a cork dork who managed two wine shops," he recalls. When things got social, Tor would cook dinner, his friend would invite fellow wine lovers and "it was epiphany after epiphany." Kenward remembers that his friends brought incredible wines to their dinners, and encouraged him to come along to Napa and Sonoma on buying trips for the stores. The rest, as they say, is history.

"I started going up to Napa in the mid-70s," he says, and moved there permanently in 1977 when he was offered a job at Beringer. "Talk about the best job in the world," he smiles. "I stayed there 27 years as Vice President of many of their most exciting programs. Kid in a candy factory."

Spend almost three decades at a winery of Beringer's caliber, and you soak up the deepest winemaking concepts and aspirations. Helping to shape Beringer's Reserve wine and culinary programs doesn't hurt, either.

"Working to make the best possible wine from raw ingredients has always been a love of mine, so all these decades as a vintner have never really seemed like work." He aimed high from the beginning, deciding that the mass market bargain wines were not what he wanted to make. He retired from Beringer and, like others before him, decided to "do his own thing."

"When I launched TOR Kenward Family wines, there was never a second thought; all the wines were going to be Reserve quality and focused on single vineyard expression." The oldest joke in the wine world is about how you make a small fortune in the wine business by starting with a large one. Fortunately, Kenward left Beringer with the resources to realize his "reserve quality" ambition.

"Thankfully, the critics blessed our first wines, and many customers have become long term supporters," he reflects. His talents, and his good reviews, gave him the ability to secure fruit from the best Cabernet and Chardonnay blocks of land in the world. The name Beckstoffer comes immediately to mind, and fruit from those ethereal vineyards makes up two of his top offerings: the TOR To Kalon Vineyard Cabernet, and the To Kalon Vineyard Red. He also makes distinguished single-vineyard wines from the Tierra Roja and Cimarossa Vineyards, among others.

He feels strongly about his best wines from Napa and Sonoma. "Our Chardonnays are $60. The Cabernet Sauvignons begin at $80 and go to $150. If we don't like something along the way we don't bottle it. Our customers get only the best, and I treat them exactly how I would like to be treated if I were on my own mailing list."

Speaking of mailing lists, most of the Kenward wines go to customers lucky enough to obtain a spot. However, he does set aside enough of his production to get into important wine markets, so more enthusiasts can discover them.

Of course, anyone who produces wine in the "reserve" range has to be sensitive to what wine critics think — and what they write in the major magazines, newsletters, and websites. Kenward's wines have scored consistently in the mid-to-upper 90s range, and some even 95 points and above. He believes that some of his wines could achieve 100 points.

"I think wine ratings can create excitement, and help small wineries such as ours move forward when they don't have sales, marketing, or PR consultants or employees." He does believe that the top critics try very hard to be fair and true to their palates, but the real question for the consumer is "which critics like the types of wines I like." His best advice: find a retail outlet with people who will listen to you intently and introduce you to new and exciting wines that may not get reviewed. "You are your own best wine critic," he maintains.

The philosophy in Kenward's winery is simple: Study the little things about each vintage. Learn how to let the personality of each vineyard take center stage. Maximize the potential of the land in every bottle. And most of all, know when to take your hands off, step back from the process, and let nature – and the fruit and the land – do the talking.

Dave Phinney --
The Mad Blender of Napa Valley

One of the things I like best about the world of wine is that you can divide it in half in a number of ways. Old World and New World. Reds and whites. Still and sparkling. One other way to split things up is by wines that are 100% somethingorother, and wines that are blended. If you're a blended wine fan, then Dave Phinney is the winemaker for you.

But first, a caution. A lot of wines are blended, even though that fact is not disclosed on the label. For example, if you buy a bottle that says "Cabernet Sauvignon" in nice big letters, the law (at least in the US) specifies that 85% of the grapes used must be the named varietal. The other 15% can be Merlot, some white wine, chocolate milk, whatever. They don't have to tell you. Staying with this example, Merlot is customarily blended with Cabernet Sauvignon to make it a bit softer and more approachable when it's young. But you might never know it by reading the label.

Similarly, it's common for Australian winemakers to put about 5% Viognier (a white wine) into their Shiraz, for a variety of reasons. But that's not the kind of blending we're talking about here.

Many regions of the world use traditional blends of several grapes. Bordeaux, for example, is generally a mixture of four to five different red wines. In Châteauneuf du Pape in the Southern Rhone, law and tradition allow as many as *thirteen* grapes in the blend, though hardly anyone uses all of them. But that's not the subject of this article, either.

Champagne, also, is generally a blend of Chardonnay, Pinot Noir, and Pinot Meuniere, so this whole blending thing is nothing new.

But here, we're talking about living dangerously…blending together varietals that are not only nontraditional, but downright off the wall. Like putting some chairs from Ikea around a Louis XIV table and somehow making it work. That's what Dave Phinney does, first at his Orin Swift winery, and then at a newer enterprise which we'll discuss below.

As I mentioned, in my experience there are two kinds of winemakers: those who are bound by respect for the traditions of their regions, and those who purposely go in exactly the opposite direction. Back in the day, winemakers from Old World countries like Spain, France, Italy, and Germany made wines the way their grandfathers did, and any new techniques or ideas were actively – sometimes violently -- discouraged. A winemaker in Bordeaux, for instance, would *never* consider using any grapes but the five that are dictated by centuries of custom and convention.

However, Dave Phinney takes the whole blending thing way over the top, which I already knew, but which he explained to me in greater detail when I interviewed him about his (very) unique and unconventional approach to blending.

I discovered Dave's wines many years ago when I tried a bottle of The Prisoner (blended wines have to have proprietary names if they don't contain 75% to 85% of whatever grape). It was a blend of about half Zinfandel all mixed up with bizarre varietals like Cabernet Sauvignon, Syrah, Petite Sirah, and Charbono (of all things). It was incredible, and became a big hit. Dave got inspired, and now makes wine in France, Italy, Spain, and Argentina. He's having too much fun.

His philosophy seems to be, let's take grapes that nobody has blended before, mix 'em together and see what we get. He gets some great results, and they're well worth trying.

In his new enterprise, which he calls "Locations," Phinney takes a wide variety of grapes from diverse areas of the world, pours them all together, shakes them up, and creates a line of bistro-style wines that get glowing reviews.

The hallmark of Phinney's winemaking style is his unconventional (to say the least) approach to blending not only widely different varietals, but also grapes from widespread regions.

"The first winemaker I worked with once told me that if have a bunch of good wines and you put them together, you can get one great wine. It works. Most of the time."

His foray into unorthodox blending started in 2000. "I had some Zinfandel with high residual sugar, a Cabernet that didn't meet my expectations, and some small lots of Syrah. I didn't want to bottle them separately, so I mixed them together." The result? A wine he called The Prisoner...and it put him on the charts.

"The success of my first wine gave me a lot of encouragement. I like to experiment with different varietals. Of course, it doesn't always work out, but look at it this way. Imagine if a chef used only one ingredient – the food wouldn't be very interesting. So for me there are no rules, no vintages, no appellations. I'll consider any grape from any region, though in my blends one varietal is usually predominant."

Like many winemakers, Phinney has mixed feelings about critics' wine ratings. "If you get a good rating, read it once, then throw it away. If you get a bad rating, read it once, then throw it away." He does believe, however, that ratings can be a guide for consumers who are not well versed, or are new to the wine world. "There are so many wines, and so many regions. Nobody can know them all."

Peter Thompson – At the Top of Diamond Mountain

People who dive into the (always risky) winemaking business come to it from all sorts of directions. Peter Thompson, who has had careers as a schoolteacher (in the Watts section of Los Angeles), an apprentice geologist, and finally an attorney, found his true calling atop Napa Valley's Diamond Mountain.

He got there the way many winemakers do – half by accident and half by design.

"I first came to the Napa Valley in September 1973, as a freshman in college," he remembers. "I was dragged there by two future fraternity brothers who really only wanted a driver so they could go wine tasting." Even though he didn't drink any wine on the trip (an omission he regrets), he fell in love with the area. And why not? Harvest was in full swing, and that's always an exciting time to be in Napa Valley.

A few years later, Thompson started sampling and learning about wine. "By the time I was a senior at USC, I had a 'substantial' wine collection: twelve bottles under my bed at the fraternity house. And some of them cost as much as $9!"

After he graduated, the frequency of his Napa visits increased to two or three times a month. Finally, after looking at over 250 properties, in August of 1995, he bought land to be planted to vines.

Andrew Geoffrey wines, named after Thompson's two sons, have collected rave reviews ever since he started producing them in 1999. He bought 66 acres and started off with 13 under vine. The property is just below the peak of Diamond Mountain, commanding a spectacular view of Napa Valley, and that's not even the best thing about it. The land is perfect for growing the kind of grapes required to produce high-quality Cabernet Sauvignon. In addition, he grows and produces a rich Cabernet Franc and deep Petit Verdot.

When Thompson talks about the quality of his wines, compromise is not an option. "From the very first, I promised myself that I'd spend the time and money necessary in the vineyard to grow the highest quality grapes possible. Wine is 90% grown, 10% made."

Winemaking style? Thompson says he doesn't have one. "I don't care what I made last year or what I will make the following year. The idea is to make the best possible wine in each vintage."

His first wine, a 2000 Cabernet Sauvignon, was released in 2004 at $75 a bottle. He kept the price constant for ten years, until the very small 2010 release, which produced only 240 cases. Today the wine sells for $85 per bottle, a modest price, considering the quality.

According to Thompson, "Andrew Geoffrey is still the lowest priced estate wine from the Diamond Mountain District."

In his mind, relationships with his customers are supremely important, which is why he converted from a distribution-based business model to a primarily direct-to-consumer approach. "I began to see the distributors buying far less and taking much longer to pay for what they did buy. So, I took steps to establish personal relationships with the people who buy my wine."

Like many owners of small wineries, Thompson travels the country building his brand – and his consumer base -- one customer at a time. Of course, that's the most time consuming and expensive way to go about it, but it does build loyalty to the wines he produces. "My customers know they can always call, text, or email me if they have a problem or simply want to know what to pair with a particular dinner entrée."

He's in step with a growing number of small winery producers regarding the efficacy of wine ratings.

"I stopped submitting wines for ratings by the so-called experts with the 2002 vintage. My only interest now is what my customers think of the wines."

Judging by his success, and the length of the waiting list for his wine club, his customers think very highly, indeed.

Is Mike Grgich "The King of Chardonnay"?

His name is Miljenko Grgich, but everybody calls him Mike, for apparent reasons. And, since 2016 was the 40th anniversary of the so-called "Judgment of Paris," it's time you get to know him...and his wines.

If you've seen the movie *Bottle Shock,* you know that the famous blind tasting held in Paris in 1976 consisted of a lineup of American and French wines sampled blind by a panel of France's most distinguished connoisseurs and critics. In the red category, six of the top ten winners were American, including Stag's Leap, Clos du Val, and Ridge Montebello. In fact, several of the judges ranked two of the American wines in first and second place against the finest Bordeaux.

In the white wine judging, three of the top four wines were American, including the #1 Chardonnay, Chateau Montelena. Though the movie does not disclose this, Mike Grgich, working at Montelena at the time, made that wine. The event put American wines squarely on the world stage, and Mike was a big part of it, even though he says he had no idea a blind tasting was happening in Paris.

"I was winemaker and limited partner at Montelena," he recalls, "but was not told by Mr. Barrett about the event." He continues that in the previous year the estate's 1972 Chardonnay "won over three best French Chardonnays at a tasting in San Diego."

"I knew it was something important when a reporter from *The New York Times* called to say they were sending a photographer to take my picture! Imagine! A little immigrant named Mike Grgich was to be in a famous New York newspaper. I started dancing around the winery and singing in Croatian that I was born again! It was a miracle!"

Mike also remembers that the prize-winning Chardonnay sold, at the time, for $6.50 a bottle.

Today, there's one bottle on display in the Smithsonian Museum to commemorate the event.

The results of the Paris tasting changed his life. "As soon as the story was released, I started getting offers to become a winemaker," he told me. "But I had always wanted to own my own winery. I had a five-year agreement that ended in 1977 and I told Mr. Barrett that I would be leaving at the end of the contract. I earned one percent ownership for each year I was winemaker at Chateau Montelena and I took the money from that to purchase land in Rutherford."

The rest, as they say, is wine world history. Today, Grgich Hills Estate produces a wide assortment of wines from classic varietals, at several different (and attractive) price points.

"I have always thought acid is important in white wines, says Grgich. Our wines are dry, crisp, balanced, food friendly, aromatic, not too oaky." He wants his wines to "give a lingering enjoyment."

They do.

Ted Seghesio – The Wizard of Zin

I've written quite often about Zinfandel, because it's one of my personal favorites. We call it "America's wine" because it's really found a home here in the US, especially in California, and is probably the most characteristic, truly American wine. Even though it originated in Croatia, and even though the Italians make it and call it Primitivo, American winemakers have really brought it to its full potential.

Ted Seghesio is one of those. His winemaking heritage in Sonoma County goes back to his great grandfather, and even though Zinfandel isn't the only wine his family makes, it's the varietal that does it for me.

Let's be honest. You don't lay Zinfandel down in the cellar for 30 years and you probably won't break out a bottle to celebrate your 50th anniversary. But for barbecues, cookouts, tailgate parties, and spicy, flavorful foods, it's what you want. It's a fun wine, so big and red and bold it can turn your teeth purple. Generally, it's packed with fruit and when it's well balanced even relatively generous levels of alcohol are undetectable.

Back to Ted. His family started out generations ago growing grapes and selling bulk wine to other producers. He went his own way for a while, and when he rejoined the business in 1983, he saw the need to produce a group of wines that could compete in what he calls "a highly competitive business environment."

"One wine," Ted remembers, "was produced by our neighbors, the Rafanellis. It was the model we aspired to." The Seghesios were impressed by the "clarity, concentration and complexity" of Rafanelli Zinfandel. Ted says, "Those are the three attributes we strive to exhibit in our wines today."

The winery is located in northern Sonoma County, where a relatively warm climate allows full ripening of the grapes. "We accentuate ripening, waiting as long as possible to harvest and not a day later," Ted explains. "The key is good acidity, which allows the fruit to retain its aromatic freshness." And, by the way, the right amount of acidity offsets and balances the sugar and alcohol content. Ask any winemaker the most important quality of a good wine, and they'll all say the same thing: balance.

One of the things I always ask winemakers in an interview is what they think about wine ratings from critics and consumer wine magazines. A rating of 90 or more points on the 100-point scale can do a lot to drive sales. A bad rating can leave you with a lot of bottles that'll never sell.

"Wine ratings help validate our efforts in the vineyards and winery," Ted says, "but we don't consider them that important. We care much more about our five generations of growing grapes and making wine that tells the story about how special Sonoma County is."

And he's right.

The Tilleys Come Home

Finding people who were actually born and raised in Napa Valley isn't as difficult as finding a native Floridian, but it's close. Some wine country natives are the children of people who have owned wineries for decades (generations, even) grew up in the vineyards, and went into the family business.

Not Chris Tilley. Born in Napa Valley, he went to St. Helena High School, then, for some insane reason, left the area to seek his fortune in the larger world. After finding it, he came back with his absolutely charming wife Pauline, bought 8 acres on St. Helena Highway, and (surprise!) planted grapevines. Good ones.

He also bought what is known in the local vernacular

as a "ghost winery." This bears a bit of explanation, because they're mostly not haunted, but Chris and Pauline swear that their place is.

On October 29, 1919, Congress overrode President Wilson's veto of the Volstead Act, and Prohibition became the law of the land. We all know how *that* turned out. One of the effects, predictably enough, was to put almost every winery in the country out of business. Many of the owners simply locked up with all the equipment in place, walked away, and let the property fall into ruin. Chris and Pauline bought one of those.

When V Madrone was established in 1883, it was a country resort, and owner August Hersch produced Cabernet Sauvignon on the property. After Prohibition, the resort became a lodge and restaurant, and passed from hand to hand until the Tilleys acquired it in 2001.

"We first saw the property the day after we were married," Chris remembers. "There was an ad about it in the local newspaper and we rushed over there immediately." The original 1880s facility, including guest cottages and barrel room, hadn't been used as a winery since Prohibition, and the Tilleys found the opportunity irresistible.

Here's the good part. In a rare moment of bureaucratic generosity, the Napa County authorities allowed the Tilleys to reactivate the original 19th Century winery permit. There were strings attached, of course, such as limiting the number of tasting room visitors and requiring them to make advance appointments, but Chris and Pauline jumped at the chance anyway.

They spent twelve years restoring the 8 acres and planting 3.5 of them with primo Cabernet Sauvignon. They restored the barrel room and winery, and cranked up production. They started an ambitious program of producing estate Cabernet Sauvignon, plus Chardonnay, old vine Zinfandel, and old vine Petite Sirah from Napa Valley vineyards owned by long-time family friends.

When they took the plunge, Pauline forsook her career as a deputy general counsel at an S&P 500 financial services company, and Chris put aside his position as a financial services executive in the property casualty industry. They actually made the move back to Napa Valley in 2008 when the economy, as Chris puts it, "was not so great. Many wineries were suffering." They persisted anyway.

From the start, the Tilleys dedicated themselves to a simple philosophy. "We make the best that we can by our standards of what we like for each of the four varietals," says Pauline. "Our winemaker knows he has to make the best without regard to cost. We want each of our varietals to express the finest of the vineyard and the terroir. That's why each of our wines is sourced from unique single sites."

Since V Madrone makes only about 2,000 cases a year, there's no national distribution. Still, the wine is easy to acquire by email, telephone, or (the best way), visiting the winery.

They established a large wine club, allocation programs, and recently began exporting to four of the largest cities in Japan. "One of the nicest developments that ever happened to us," says Chris, "was when we were invited to participate in the Southwest Florida Wine Fest many years ago. Now it's one of the top five charity wine events in America."

The Guigals -- First Families of Wine

In many ways, winemaking can be very much of a family business. A lot of people get born into it, like Piero Antinori in Italy, whose family has been making wine for over 700 years, and who owns an impressive chunk of downtown Florence. The Mondavi brothers, Peter and Robert, are another good example.

We might not be that familiar with family dynasties in other countries, but in France, the Guigals should certainly come to mind. In a recent interview, Phillipe Guigal told me a bit about his family's (fairly recent) history. But since they have their name on a hilltop in the Northern Rhône, and since they produce wines at prices that run from great values to you gotta be kidding me, the wines, and the people who make them, deserve our attention.

"We are a relatively young company," says Phillipe. The story begins with his grandfather, Etienne Guigal, who founded the firm in 1945. Later, he handed the company over to his son Marcel, Phillipe's father, who celebrated his 55th vintage in 2015.

In the Northern Rhône, the major traditional red grape is Syrah, and pretty much only Syrah, from vineyards in Côte-Rôtie, Saint Joseph, Hermitage and Crozes-Hermitage. The Guigals make whites from the heritage Viognier, Marsanne, and Roussanne grapes. Phillipe is adamant that the family makes wine only in this region. "We feel that we could not control the quality in the way that we want if we tried to make wine in another region in France, let alone another country."

At the age of 22, Phillipe took over as winemaker for the family business, and he carries on what he calls his grandfather's "simple vision": to make the highest quality wines possible, farming organically and without pesticides. And even though many of the Guigal single vineyard offerings, like La Turque, La Mouline, and La Landonne (known in the wine world as "The La-Las") will hit you for over $500 a bottle, many others are available at extremely attractive prices.

"We are the birthplace of two of the great red grapes in the world: Syrah and Grenache," states Phillipe. "These have been brought to other parts of France and the world, and we love many versions and interpretations, but truly the Rhône Valley is the home of these grapes." While Bordeaux has Cabernet and Merlot, and Burgundy has Pinot Noir, the Rhône Valley has its own unique traditional varietals that age beautifully, but can be enjoyed young as well.

Unlike many producers, the Guigals tend to hold their wines for quite a while before releasing them. Says Phillipe, "When you have great material, time is the key for the elements to come together, and for complexity to develop. Our wines are drinking at an optimum level when they are released. That is one of the major reasons consumers come back to our wines again and again."

Greg Brewer Heads for the Hills

At a wine tasting in Miami Beach, I had the chance to chat with winemaker Greg Brewer. His Brewer-Clifton winery is recognized as one of the finest producers of Pinot Noir and Chardonnay in the Santa Barbara district. Specifically, he farms over 80 acres in the Sta. Rita appellation, and his wines consistently earn 90+ points from critics. His 2012 Pinot Noir was #8 on Wine Spectator's Top 100 list of 2014.

He and his original partner Steve Clifton put together $10,000 to establish their winery in 1996 and he currently farms the four distinctive vineyards he owns. Today, partnering with Master Sommelier Ken Fredrickson, the winery produces four single vineyard Chardonnays and six Pinot Noirs in the Sta. Rita Hills appellation outside Santa Barbara. The annual production is around 10,000 cases.

Originally a French instructor at the University of Santa Barbara, Brewer began working in Sta. Rita in the 1990s as an assistant in a winery, and "became seduced by the incredible winegrowing area." He made it his goal to produce his own wines in the district. "What really attracted me," he remembers, "was the fact that every wine I produce will be different. There's a certain humility in never being able to reproduce one's work."

Even though Pinot Noir is known as the "heartbreak grape" because it's so difficult to grow, Brewer dived in. "The challenge is the most interesting part of the process," he maintains. He ferments whole clusters, with no destemming because the stems moderate the sweetness of the Pinot Noir. And interestingly enough, the oak barrels he uses are up to 15 years old. According to Brewer, the wines should be in a "neutral state," with no additives and as little interference from the winemaker as possible.

"I'm after the pure flavors of the wine," he says. "I want to remove the winemaker's signature. At our winery it's not about what we do to the wine...it's about what we don't do." Like every other winemaker I've met, Brewer insists on respecting and focusing on the place where the grapes come from. "We handle the fruit from each vineyard identically from harvest to bottling. This allows the true essence of the site to best be expressed."

Ultimately, it was announced that Brewer had sold his winery to Jackson Family Wines, a worldwide company that owns literally dozens of wineries across the globe.

"I've always been dedicated to my work," says Brewer of the acquisition, "and I'll still be at the helm of Brewer-Clifton as full-time winemaker and brand ambassador."

With Brewer remaining in charge, there's no doubt that his wines will maintain their reputation for quality and purity they've enjoyed over the past 20 years. If you see them on the shelf, buy them.

Sarah Marquis -- The New Face of Australian Wine

Since 2005, Sarah and Sparky Marquis have produced stunning world-class wines in McLaren

Vale, Australia. Their winery is named Mollydooker, which is Australian slang for a left-handed person. Sort of like our "southpaw."

Since they started, the couple's bold red wines garnered outstanding ratings from critics all over the world, and still do. Their Carnival of Love Shiraz was *Wine Spectator* Number 2 Wine of the Year in 2016, and many of their other brands have received outstanding ratings.

Recently, however, a break-up between the two has left Sarah as the sole owner of the world-renowned winery, and the new face of the brand. Since the beginning, Sparky, personable and outgoing, served as the brand ambassador. Now it's Sarah's turn, and it's apparent she's up to the task.

We've known the couple for many years, and I had a chance to spend some time with Sarah at the New York Wine Experience in October, 2017. Supported by her father-in-law and her son Luke (who's just turned 21) she's more than confident in her ability to guide the winery – and the brands – into the future.

"We're absolutely going to maintain our unique style," she says. "The wine's intensity on the palate is very important." Sarah and her winemaking team measure intensity by what they uniquely call "fruit weight," a sensory term that embodies the velvety sensation of the wine on the palate, and its concentration.

As sole owner, Sarah plans to continue and build on the brand's somewhat irreverent approach to the way their wines are named...and handled.

First, the names. Mollydooker has always been

famous for its somewhat puckish approach. Their wines are called "Barefoot Boy," "Velvet Glove," "Carnival of Love," "Enchanted Path"...and that's just scratching the surface. And then they invented the "Mollydooker Shake" as a way to make wine open up and "breathe." Most of us would carefully uncork our bottles, and pour the wine gently into a decanter, being careful not to agitate it or "bruise" the delicate liquid. Not these people.

At lunch with Sarah and Sparky in McLaren Vale a few years ago, we were treated to a demonstration of the Mollydooker Shake. Sparky opened a bottle of their highly-rated Carnival of Love, poured about three ounces into one of the glasses, replaced the cork and gave the bottle a vigorous and punishing shake. He poured another glass, and we tasted the unshaken wine next to the one that had been mistreated. Night and day. The shaken wine was much more open, fruity, and accessible. Sarah fully intends to carry on that tradition.

In fact, she had an event called "Mollydooker at Sea"...a cruise out of Miami on the Celebrity Equinox in June of 2018. Passengers joined Sarah for what she described as the "ultimate Mollydooker experience," a seven-night Caribbean voyage filled with intimate tastings, blending classes, and wine lunches and dinners.

While some of Sarah's wines, such as the highly-rated Velvet Glove, run into the $150 range, the big bold Carnival of Love and Enchanted Path Shirazes can be found for around $60...and worth every nickel. Fortunately, the winery produces several quite pleasing wines for daily enjoyment, such as Two Left Feet red blend, The Maitre D' Merlot, and The Boxer Shiraz are available for well under $25 each. So there's no reason to wait...the wines are widely available (though joining the wine club is always a good idea) and undoubtedly world class.

It's All in the Glass

I confess that I don't need a lesson in how the type of glass affects the taste of wine. Debi and I have been to enough tastings, and sipped from dozens of different glasses. Plus, at the Wine Experience a few years ago, Georg and Maximilian Riedel demonstrated the difference to about 1500 of us. We tasted a wine out of a plastic cup, then out of several differently-shaped Riedel glasses, and the variation in the aromas and flavors was obvious to everyone in the room.

So the glass makes a difference – and quite often a major one.

The Riedel name has been synonymous with fine wine glasses since the 1750s. (By the way, it rhymes with "needle.") In 1973, Claus Riedel (the 9th generation of the glassmaking family) introduced the "Sommelier Series," the first mouth-blown glasses made to pair wines with a specific bowl shape. He was also the first designer to discover that the bouquet and flavors of a wine were affected by the shape of the bowl.

The company conducts extensive research to determine what shapes are best for different wines. Company President Georg Riedel told me that the process involves "a series of trial and error tastings," something I'd very much like to participate in. "Working with winemakers and sommeliers, we tweak the bowl shape and rim diameter to deliver wine in a fashion that best accentuates the properties of the given varietal on the taster's palate," he says. "Within each glassware series, there are shapes for the world's major wine varietals, including bowl shapes for new world and old world wines."

Anyone who buys and uses Riedel glasses soon discovers one thing about this company's glassware – it's hilariously fragile. My mother-in-law once dropped an ice cube into one of them, and it went all the way through and out the bottom. I told that to Georg.

"Riedel is known for creating some of the thinnest glasses on the market," he responded. "But we make numerous glassware lines that stand up to everyday wear and tear, both for home enjoyment and professional hospitality use."

Another breakthrough that Riedel is known for is the "O" series of glasses. These have the correct bowl shape for wine, but are stemless. We've found them to be excellent for traveling, and they're dishwasher safe.

Mr. Riedel also explained to me the process behind finding the perfect glass shape for different wine varietals. "My son Maximilian and I conduct extensive workshops before a varietal-specific shape can make it to market. We follow the Bauhaus principle: form follows function."

But surely, differences in the way individuals experience a certain wine must play a part? "Yes," says Georg Riedel. "There is a degree of individuality to each person's interpretation of a wine, but most sensory responses are directly affected by the vessel. This doesn't erase personal preference; there are those who simply prefer Pinot Noir to Cabernet Sauvignon. But we firmly believe that each varietal will taste its absolute best when served in a Riedel glass."

At our house, we conduct numerous side-by-side tastings. Every night, in fact. It's hard to disagree with Georg.

PART IV
THE WORLD OF WINE

*A*side from water, wine is one of our most ancient beverages. Way back when, water and milk could kill you. Wine, however, made a hard life a bit more bearable. Same today.

The topics in this section don't fall into any specific category. There is so much information about various aspects of wine and its place in our cultures and our lives (and our religions, even) that thoughts tend to wander all over the place.

For example, there has been a lot of crosstalk in the wine media over the past few years about the expanding role of women in the wine trade, as winemakers, reviewers and critics, marketers, and major consumers. Similarly, writers and buyers have been paying a good deal of attention to issues like the effects of global warming on wine production, the rise of dozens of wine clubs, alternative containers like cans and boxed wine, screwcaps vs corks, and a lot more.

So as those issues have come up in trade journals and seminars, and as they've attracted attention, I've dug in to them, talked to people, and nosed around. The following essays are the result of an unceasing – and sometimes unhealthy – curiosity.

Cork Dorks and Grape Geeks

One day, countless thousands of years ago, somebody put a bunch of grapes into some kind of bowl. The fruit got crushed and the yeast on the skins acted on the juice, which spoiled in the most delightful way. Thanks to the accident of fermentation, a lot of people got happy.

The making of wine is an incredibly ancient pursuit. Thousands, even only hundreds of years ago, any other beverage would probably kill you. Drinking water came from the stream where wild animals bathed (and performed other functions), and once humans figured out how to get raw milk from animals, that was mostly lethal, too.

Over time, wine became a sacrament to some of the world's major religions, and, in the last thousand years or so, has become part of what we usually call the finer things in life. Wine is a cultural artifact, and it communicates something about where the grapes were grown and about the people who made it.

Since winemaking has been practiced for well over three thousand years (almost certainly more), the world of wine has become a very big place. The topic fascinates many of us, but there's always a danger that fascination can become obsession, and then...snobbery. People become cork dorks. It's not a good thing.

It's a well-recognized danger of the wine life: a practically inevitable propensity to become a grape geek. Any hobby, passion, or obsession we pursue takes up a chunk of our lives, and when we get jacked about something, we want to share. Those who succumb to and pursue an interest in wine can sooner or later become the same way, only worse.

But on the other hand, a bit of wine knowledge and understanding can be rewarding. It brings to us what we bring to it, so why not bring as much as we can?

Problem is, cork dorks who discourse over dinner about the 500-year history of what's in the bottle can become boring at best. And if you ever hear somebody say "it's a naïve little Burgundy without much breeding, but I'm sure you'll be amused by its presumption," well, no jury in the world will convict you if you shoot him.

There are hundreds of grape varietals, and hundreds of places – some well-known and some quite obscure – where wine is made. You don't need to be able to name the ten wine districts of Beaujolais, or the five wines allowed in the Bordeaux blend, to increase your understanding and appreciation, but a little effort – and a little knowledge -- can go a long way toward adding to your enjoyment.

We're all faced with the problem of looking at a restaurant wine list, or gazing upon the selection in a wine store, and trying to figure out what to try next. Fact is, no consumer product in the world gives us less information than the label on a wine bottle. About all producers are required to list is their name, the place where it's made, how much is in the bottle, and the alcohol content. Not even the name of the grape. This causes a lot of aspiring wine lovers to throw up their hands in disgust and go back to beer.

The solution? Sample widely. Read a bit. Go to tastings and wine dinners where people speak about the wines being poured. My favorite introductory book (aside from my own *Secrets of the Wine Whisperer*) is *The Wine Bible* by Karen MacNeil. Also *Great Wine Made Simple* by Andrea Immer Robinson. Excellent places to start.

What Does Oak Do To Wine?

There are two plants essential to winemaking: the grapevine and the oak tree. Since most wine is either fermented in oak or aged in it, maybe it would be good to know why...and what kind of flavors and sensations we can expect from wine that's been "oaked."

When you start making wine, you're faced with a ton of decisions: which grapes to plant and where to plant them, when to harvest, what style of wine to make, what kind of container for fermentation and aging. It goes on and on. For the moment, let's forget about the grape stuff and concentrate on the whole container issue. That's where all the oak comes in.

For fermentation and aging, you'll choose either oak barrels or stainless steel tanks (or some other neutral container), for very specific reasons. Why oak? When the liquid is in contact with oak, the wine softens and soaks up several flavor components. The effects are very different for red wines and whites. Second, the choice of which kind of oak (and how the barrels are made) has a dramatic influence on flavor, color, spoilage, and other characteristics.

Sometimes, the back label of a wine bottle will carry a statement like "aged for 14 months in new American oak." That's important, because different kinds of oak impart different kinds of flavors, and knowing which is which can help you guess what kind of drinking experience you might be in for.

We can conveniently divide the whole oak issue into two – or maybe four – parts. You, as a winemaker, will choose either French or American oak, and then decide whether to buy new barrels (at about $1,500 a pop) or ones that have been used once or twice. Used barrels impart more subtle flavors, and they're cheaper.

Depending on how a barrel is made, different types of flavors will be absorbed into the wine. The process of making barrels is called cooperage, so if you know anyone named Cooper, chances are that barrel making is what their distant ancestors did for a living.

Barrels are made over heat, which allows the staves to be bent into the proper shapes. When fire is used, the sugars in the wood are caramelized, imparting flavors of coffee, chocolate, vanilla, toffee, and toasted nuts, among others. That's why those types of barrels are generally used for big reds such as Cabernet Sauvignon, Merlot, Zinfandel, and Syrah.

But when the same types of barrels are used for a white wine like Chardonnay, rich flavors of vanilla and oak itself leach into the wine. In fact, the "oaky" style of Chard was very much in fashion not long ago. Today, tastes have shifted toward the "unoaked" style, which delivers more of the pure fruit flavors and the zing of acidity. Many times, the front or back label will tell you whether the wine is unoaked.

The major sources for wine barrel oak are France, the US, and sometimes Hungary. American oak is loose-grained, and the resulting flavors are bolder and more obvious. French oak imparts more subtle flavors.

Depending on how much of those oak flavors you want in your wine, you might choose to do the actual fermentation in large oak vats, then transfer the wine into smaller barrels for aging. (The size of the aging barrel also affects flavor, but that's another story). Then you'll figure out how long to mature it in the barrel, tasting it from time to time to see how it's coming along. Barrel sampling is one of my favorite things.

Since barrels are so expensive, some winemakers take the cheap route, and get the oak characteristics into their wine by simply throwing oak chips into the vat. I hate it when that happens.

Some wines have back labels that actually give you some real information. If you find one, remember that most top quality red wines benefit from oak, as do white Burgundies and many Chardonnays. Naturally, new oak imparts stronger flavors than oak that has been used a few times. In red wines, look for those overtones of vanilla, caramel, clove, smoke, and cinnamon. In whites, you can expect toasted almond, nutmeg, allspice, and other yummies.

Wine Bottle Back Labels – Help or Hype?

As I always tell my wine classes, there is no consumer product that gives a buyer less information about what's in the container than a wine label. You can go into a supermarket, pick up a box of corn flakes, and be treated to an encyclopedic summary of every single ingredient in the box, including nutrition information, how many milligrams of salt, protein, sugar, carbohydrates, chemicals, all of it. But none of that appears on a wine bottle, because it's not required. How they get away with it is a mystery.

On the front, you'll see the name of the producer, maybe the grape varietal, maybe the region where the grapes were grown, alcohol content (more or less), and how much is in the bottle. That's about it.

But the back label? I've studied them extensively (not having much of a life) and that's a whole different story. Basically, I've divided them into two categories: the hype label and the help label. The hype label is much more common.

Actually, most bottles have two back labels, but one just tells you not to drink the wine if you're planning to get pregnant and operate heavy machinery. I follow that caution to the letter. The other label, however, is where things get sticky.

The first type is the hype label: a paragraph of shamelessly promotional copy that tells you how great the wine is and why you should buy it at once. Winemakers write about how their family harvests the grapes one by one...how they weep with joy as they crush and blend the final product...and how this delicious wine is a perfect accompaniment to any type of cuisine and should be enjoyed every day and every night. Yadda, yadda.

The help label, however, is much to be respected and sought after. Winemakers who are smart enough to tell me what's in the bottle will get my money first, every time. At least let me know what the blend is, and if you're really good you'll give me the percentages of the Zinfandel, Counoise, Charbono, Aglianico and whatever else you threw in there. That way, I might know what kind of flavors and aromas to expect. Maybe you'll tell me if the wine was aged in oak, what kind, and for how long, so I'll get a little preview of what to look for as I swirl, sniff, and slurp.

Winemaker Paul Draper, whose Ridge label is very highly regarded (and rated), is almost single-handedly fighting this trend. His labels include all sorts of information On the front label, he lists the exact blend. His Geyserville red is 78% Zinfandel, 16% Carignane, 4% Petite Sirah, 1% Alicante Bouschet, and 1% Mourvedre. On the back he lists the ingredients: Hand harvested, sustainably grown grapes, indigenous yeasts, naturally occurring malolactic bacteria, calcium carbonate, minimum effective SO_2"

What to take away from all this? First, if you're not familiar with the particular producer, a helpful back label might convince you to buy the bottle. This is especially true if the wine has a proprietary name, like Insignia, Alexis, or Promontory, something like that. If there's a grape name on the label (as there probably will be if the wine comes from North or South America, Australia, New Zealand, or South Africa) you may get a hint if it's something you want to try. But if the bottle does not contain 75%-85% of one particular grape (depending on where it's from), the winemaker has to call it something else. In that case, it can be especially helpful if the particular blend is listed. If it's not, be adventurous. Buy it anyway. If you like it, you can always go back and get more.

How to Taste Wine Like a Pro -- The "5-S Approach"

A lot of people enjoy wine, but not all of them appreciate it. There's a difference. Enjoying wine means liking it. *Appreciating* wine means knowing *why* you like it.

Drinking wine is a lot like listening to a symphony orchestra. First, you get the total impact of the music – all of the instruments play together, and they all hit you at once. But as you learn to *appreciate* music, you start to pick out the sounds of the individual instruments and understand how they work together to produce the total effect.

Same with wine. First, you get the overall sensations of aroma and taste, but as you learn the process, you start to distinguish – and understand – the individual flavor components. When I gather my tasting panel friends to help me review wines for my columns, we use a specific evaluation method I call the "5-S Approach." It's a professional process, and the gateway to greater enjoyment and more fun with the wines you share with friends. So try this the next time you pull a cork or twist a cap.

1] SEE – Look at the wine by holding the glass a bit sideways over a light surface. The color can tell the age and condition of the wine. Reds lose color as they age, turning a dull brown or brick. Whites gain color, going from yellow to gold to brown. Opacity is important. The darker it is, the more full-bodied it will be on the palate.

2] SWIRL – Keep the glass on the table and swirl the wine. This aerates the liquid, releasing aromatic and flavor components.

3] SNIFF – This is a critical step, because 85% of our sense of taste is actually smell. Put your nose way down inside the glass, close your eyes, and take a few short sniffs, like a puppy. What's the first thing that comes to your mind? In white wines, do you smell white or yellow fruit? In reds, are there aromas of red or black cherries, plums, or berries? Or do you get hit up front with earth scents like tobacco, smoke, cedar, leather, or similar sensations?

4] *SIP* – When you sip, suck some air into the wine through your front teeth, then "chew" the liquid around in your mouth a bit. This exposes all the sensors on your tongue to the full range of flavors. Again, think of the very first taste that comes to your mind. Then think of the second...and the third.

5] *SWALLOW* – When you swallow, be aware of how long the flavors linger on your palate and in the back of your mouth. This is the "finish," and the longer you sense the flavors, the better the wine is likely to be. Of course, when we're sipping through 15 to 20 wines at a sitting, we don't swallow them all. That's where the spit bucket comes in. If you ever go to a real professional tasting session, you'll see people expectorating all over the place. You should, too, or you'll never make it home. By the way, this spitting is a muted, decorous process. It's not polite to go for distance.

So instead of gulping down your next glass of Chianti or Riesling, try this professional process. As you really pay attention to what's happening on your palate, and as you start to sense individual flavor components, you'll enjoy your wines more, and your food will start tasting better, too.

Mmmmm! These Pencil Shavings are Delicious!

Every once in a while, a wine topic flares up in the consumer and trade press and our attention is attracted. There is quite a bit written on the topic of how we talk about wine: how critics and others describe the flavors, aromas, and other sensations offered by this marvelous, mystical liquid.

Problem is, the terms they use, which are called "descriptors," often give us very little real information and are, at times, completely off the charts.

To put it bluntly, wine is nothing more than spoiled grape juice. Apple juice tastes like apples and orange juice tastes like oranges. Let either of them ferment, and the result is lousy-tasting juice that will probably kill you if you drink it. But when grape juice becomes wine the final product often tastes like anything but the fruit it's made of. As the mysterious chemical rearrangements of fermentation occur, and winemakers apply their art, the juice gives up flavors that have no resemblance to the Welch's we all grew up with.

When I first started drinking wine critically I was both shaken and stirred by the twisted tastes critics discovered as they swirled and sipped. They detected flavors in wine that I didn't even want to think about, let alone put in my mouth. And the vocabulary they used to describe the flavors is a psycholinguistic study in itself, requiring readers to come at the English language from a perspective that's more than a little out of plumb.

They talk about wine having "backbone," and "stuffing." There are wines that are "muscular," and others that are "shy" or "supple." Tannins can be "velvety." Wine can be "chunky," and "chewy," or even "jammy." It can "resonate," it can be "round," and certainly "seductive." Clearly, wine writers are especially adept at putting a little… well, English on the language.

But those words are nothing compared to the "descriptors." Here, the language soars skyward like an exultation of larks, but the flavors go in exactly the opposite direction. Just to show that I'm not making any of this up, here's a sample of actual reviews of some top-end wines that often sell for outer-spatial prices.

"…scents of underbrush, smoke, saddle leather, soy, and other assorted Asian spices begin to emerge along with kirsch liqueur and black fruit notes."

"…cooked apple, lemon, and petrol." I think that means gasoline.

"Reticent but lively aromas of black raspberry and blackberry syrup…Very expressive, super ripe flavors of plum, nuts, game and animal fur." Animal fur?

Not having much of a life my own self, I started making lists of my favorite weird wine tastes and aromas as I encountered them in the critics' reviews. Here are some examples.

Forest floor. Like wet leaves, moss, damp trees. Wine with flavors like this are far from spoiled. *Au contraire,* they cost a bundle.

Horse sweat. Goes right along with the saddle leather, if you know what I mean.

Barnyard. The bouquet of the chicken coop is unmistakable. We've never experienced it firsthand, but recognized it a lot quicker than we care to admit.

Pencil shavings. It takes you right to the second grade, and that gray crank machine screwed to the wall, full of wood and warm graphite smell. That's this.

Your impressions probably won't be as poetic, though they might. The important thing is, when you sniff and sip, immediately say the first thing that comes into your mind, no matter how screwy it might be. Then say the second, and the third. You'll be tasting like a pro in no time.

The Art of Blind Tasting

For many people (me included) the most entertaining – and maddening – activity in the wine world is a little thing called the blind tasting. It is a very special, very peculiar, form of masochism that is particular to the wine world. A blind tasting is where you have a glass (or two) of wine in front of you with no idea what kind it is, and you have to sniff, sip, and identify it. I call it the "guess the smell" contest, and it's just about impossible to do...for me at least.

There are national blind tasting contests, championships, even, where people can win free trips to the finals in Las Vegas by tasting a wine and identifying not only the varietal, but many times the place of origin, the vintage, and – most remarkable of all – the producer. Not me. Not ever.

In fact, there's a very entertaining movie called *Somm,* which is about five young men who form a study group to prepare to take the Master Sommelier exam, which is known to be more difficult than Chinese algebra. A significant component of the exam (which is held over two days) is the blind tasting. They are required to taste several wines and absolutely nail everything about them. Varietal, region, vintage, soil, maybe even the barometric pressure on the day the grapes were harvested.

I've been invited to several blind tastings, but I'd much rather watch other people sip and suffer. One such event was held to help the manager of a restaurant near our home prepare to take her Level II sommelier test, which would require her to taste two wines blind and identify them. She wanted to practice, and asked a few of us to taste along.

Her name was Jessica Weeks, and probably still is. She was raised in the Finger Lakes region of upstate New York, which is one of America's original and historic winegrowing regions. We held the practice session in the very impressive wine tasting laboratory at Florida Gulf Coast University in Fort Myers.

"I've been in the restaurant industry since I was 16 years old," she says, "but it wasn't until I joined the Guild of Sommeliers that I realized just how much goes into each bottle. It's given me a great respect for what it takes to grow and harvest grapes at the precise time to make a successful wine. It's all very fascinating."

That fascination led Jessica to prepare for her Level II exam, where she would be required to demonstrate a Wikipedic knowledge of wine varietals, regions, soils, producers, and a lot more.

"The test consists, among other things, of 40 multiple choice or short answer questions," she notes. "I also have to blind taste two wines and explain the makeup of the varietal, where it came from, how old it is, the tasting notes, if it was stored in oak or not, the climate and soil in which it was grown, and many other factors based on sight, smell, and taste."

No simple task. The first mystery wine we tasted was a white, which I immediately and confidently identified as a Reisling from Germany. Jessica said it was an Albariño from northern Spain. She was right. I was wrong. Then there was a red which I absolutely *knew* was a Pinot Noir from Burgundy. Jessica begged to differ, suggesting a Gamay from Beaujolais, which is kind of like Burgundy's twin cousin. Once again, her sipping sophistication defeated mine. Jessica two, Jerry zero.

Then, she nailed the Nebbiolo from northern Italy, along with the other two blind bottles. If anybody was ready to take the test, it was her. I had no doubt she'd be able to achieve what she described as a "personal goal." (She did).

"It will definitely make a difference in my career," she notes. "I am pursuing the more advanced certifications to become more knowledgeable and qualified when recommending wine to a restaurant guest. Most of them may know a certain type of wine they enjoy, so it's a great pleasure to introduce new styles by explaining the selections in detail."

Good luck with that. I'll stick to reading the label.

The War of the Ratings

It's a bewildering situation – how do wines get rated and scored by critics and wine magazine editors? It is, however, an ongoing issue and some information was recently published that casts a new, and very interesting, light on the topic.

First of all, I need to let you know that I have several wine friends who wouldn't dream of buying a wine rated less than 90 points. I've always thought that was insane, because I've found great values – and great sipping experiences – in wines that don't cost a whole lot and may not get that cherished 90-piont distinction. I'm happy to say that my attitude was amply supported by an article I read in *Wine Spectator* magazine. But more on that below.

If you go wine shopping, one thing is for certain: you'll be confronted by some kind of rating information. Every wine retailer puts critics' favorable wine ratings on the shelf talker, price tag, point of sale sign, somewhere. Wines that receive high ratings will trumpet that information right on the bottle with a sticker, hanger tag or some other attention-getting device. The problem is, what do the ratings actually mean, and should your purchase decisions be determined by the fact that some magazine or taster gave this wine 88 points, or 93 points? I say no.

Many years ago, when critics rated wines, they used a 20-point scale. The rationale was that there was more discernible difference between a wine rated 18 and one rated 19. Today, the 100-point scale is universal, and I dare anybody to taste the difference between an 88-point wine and one rated 89.

Even more puzzling (and disturbing) is the situation among the various wine consumer magazines, because there's no consistency in the way they assign points. As consumers we just have to figure it all out ourselves.

Case in point: I usually trust the ratings given by *Wine Spectator*, and by certain independent critics, but I don't trust *Wine Enthusiast* magazine, because they consistently rate wines two to five points higher than everybody else. I tell my wine classes that *Wine Enthusiast* never met a wine they weren't enthusiastic about. Inflated ratings don't do us any good.

So. Is a 92-point wine that much better than an 86-point wine? Is there that much difference in quality, or in the enjoyment you'll experience when you drink them?

In a recent issue, the editors of *Wine Spectator* were asked to list their personal favorite wines. Surprise. These journalist/critics, all of whom are able to sample (and buy) just about any wine in the world, listed tons of favorite wines that rated well below 90 points, and well below $20 a bottle. Now, those are the wines you want to look for.

Senior editor Bruce Sanderson selected, among others, an 88-point Bouchard Père & Fils Bourgogne

Réserve 2013 that costs just $22. Any time you can get a decent Burgundy for around that price, you buy it. James Molesworth, another editor, listed an 88-point Château Marsau Bordeaux that costs $23. So even though these critics can drink anything they want, they also can spot the values...and they don't have to be 90-pointers.

Observation: There is, admittedly, a distant relationship between how good a wine is and how much it costs. Many factors go into the pricing of a wine. How many cases do they make? How do they market the wine? Is it sold at retail, or only to those on the winery's "club" list? We buy one very limited-production wine because we're on the list...and we waited years for our names to come up. However, as soon as we receive it, it's worth about three times what we paid, so there's some investment value here, as well. An examination of the relationship between ratings and prices could fill a book all by itself.

The moral of the story is, there are only two kinds of wine: the kind you like and the kind you don't Don't be afraid to buy an 88-point wine, because it could be great.

Red Table Wine. Only $250 a Bottle.

Seems a little steep, doesn't it, to pay over $100 for a bottle of something that says "table wine" or just "red wine" on the label. It isn't one of those rare blockbuster California Cabernets, or a precious vintage from the sacred vineyards of Burgundy. It's just...well, red table wine.

But wait. Take a closer look at where it's from, and what's inside the bottle, because that humble title can conceal a drinking experience that's well worth the price. And more.

Most likely, the label you're looking at comes from Italy, or some other ancient winemaking area that's steeped in long tradition and strict custom. So if you're confused about what's in the bottle, you can thank the Italian government. Over the years, they passed a whole spate of laws defining specific wine zones in the country, decreeing what kind of "recipe" each wine should conform to, how long it should be aged, all that. Unfortunately, they forgot one thing: the most innovative winemakers may not want to follow the official recipes. That's true everywhere.

Say you're sitting out there in your vineyard in the middle of Chianti, a few miles from Castellina or some other ancient winemaking center, and you just don't want to make your wine the way the Official Recipe demands. Maybe you're feeling puckish and you throw in a little of that Cabernet you've been growing, or a couple of Merlot grapes. You've got a problem. Follow the traditional recipe, and you can call your wine Chianti. Don't, and you can't.

There's no official name for wines that don't conform, so what do you call them? Probably, you'd call them Super Tuscans, which is exactly what the major Italian producers, over the past decade or so, have done.

In the most popular – and expensive – Super Tuscans, Sangiovese is still the major grape, and the wine serves as a sensational accent to all kinds of traditional Italian cuisines. The rest (there are maybe about 20) are made from Merlot, Cabernet Sauvignon, Syrah, and other international varietals. As I said, wines from Chianti that do not follow the rules don't have an official terminology. What's worse, they get classified in the lowest designation of quality, which is called IGT, down there with the $8 bottles. The lack of an official name for nonconforming wine has driven producers to make up clever names of their own, all of which contain lots of vowels. There's Ornellaia, which is made primarily from Cabernet Sauvignon. And Tignanello, which is mostly Sangiovese. Then there's the wine that is said to have started the whole Super Tuscan revolution, Sassicaia, made from Cabernet Sauvignon and aged and barreled differently from any other Chianti regional wine up to its time.

While Super Tuscans like Solaia, Summus, or Fontalloro may cost well over a Franklin apiece, some are priced a little more mercifully. My bargain favorite, Monte Antico, is made mostly from Sangiovese, but not entirely, and costs under $15 a bottle. While it can't compare to the juice that Marchese Antinori is putting in his Tignanello bottles, it's a nice step away from your typical Chianti, and it's absolutely sensational with pizza.

What Year Is It, Anyway?

For many people, one of the most confusing things about wine appreciation is all that business about vintages. Good years, bad years, even mediocre years – it's tough to keep all that information straight in your head. Besides, does it really matter?

I've found that there's no better way to learn vintages than simply letting nature take its course: Every year, trailing the calendar by a few months to several years, each new vintage comes through the pipeline, bringing its own surprises and teaching us its particular lessons through tasting. It's a good opportunity to make a few points about vintage and its place in wine appreciation. Live through a few vintages, learn them in your glass, and before long you realize that you do have a lot of that info in your head.

But first, let's tick off a few random "bullet points" about some ways that wine lovers use -- and abuse -- information about vintages.

- Vintage, the year shown on the bottle of most fine wines, reflects the year in which the grapes were picked. Since wine grapes are an agricultural product, weather conditions can have a significant effect on the wine. For example, a summer of extreme heat in Europe can result in very ripe fruit, which may not necessarily be a blessing, as over-ripe grapes tend to make fat, lower-acid wines.

- All weather, like all politics, is local. One region's terrible vintage may be decent in another and a godsend in a third. A lackluster year in Napa may be very good in Bordeaux, or vice versa. Indeed, when we mention intense summer heat in Europe, remember that we're talking only about a certain region. Maybe that same growing season was excellent in South Africa, and "difficult" in much of California and Down Under. We need to be specific.

- Vintage quality works only as a broad generalization. Some producers make excellent wines in "poor" vintages, and a few make stinkers in "can't miss" years. Moreover, the storm or frost that devastated vines in one village may have missed its neighbor. It's rare to have a vintage so poor that consumers have to write it off entirely. The 1997 vintage in Bordeaux comes close to this mark, when even the prestigious First Growth wines were very disappointing. But now and then we can find value by cherry-picking better wines from vintages that conventional wisdom says to avoid.

- Trust your own taste buds more than vintage charts. Famous wine professionals like Robert Parker may highly rate a vintage that produced big, strong and ripe wines in France, which drives up prices. But what if you don't share his affection for bold, concentrated wines? There are only two kinds of wines: the ones you like and the ones you don't.

What's a WOTY?

Every December, *Wine Spectator* magazine publishes a list they call their "Top 100 Wines of the Year." Among my wine geek friends, we just call them WOTYs. The list includes selections by the magazine's editors, culled from the literally thousands of wines they sample and critique throughout the year. (I applied for that job. Didn't get it.)

When the list comes out, collectors all over the world race to their cellars to see how many of the Top 100 wines they have. It's a sickness.

The list is an excellent example of the classic good news/bad news joke. Good news: many of the listed wines are great values, which is the whole purpose of this chapter. Bad news: others on the list can cost as much as a mortgage payment. More bad news: the minute the list comes out, the wines fly off the shelves, so if you're not right on top of things, there won't be any left. Good news: many wines are high production so that even ordinary people like us can get some.

The list also calls into question the idea of wine ratings in general. Wines are sampled and scored on a scale of 100 points by all kinds of people and publications. Some of the critics are associated with magazines, while others work alone. Regardless, they all sample wines – hundreds of them – and tell us what they think. In short, these people have a lot of influence, and many wines live or die by the points they are assigned.

Of course, there's nothing more personal than reacting to the taste of a wine. The proof is on the palate, and everybody has one. So…if a critic gives a wine 90+ points, there's no guarantee that you or I will agree. Want proof? Come to my house, and enjoy the spirited discussions between my wife and me about which wine should be enjoyed and which should be poured down the sink. *De gustibus,* said the Romans, *non est disputandum.* Translated loosely, it means you stick to your wine ratings, and I'll stick to mine.

Another thing: it's clear that price isn't always proportional to quality. For example, the #1 Wine of the Year a few years back was rated 95 points, and cost around $55. The #50 was rated 98 points, and cost $175. Go figure.

There's more. If a wine gets a good rating – especially if it's a less-expensive bottling – the producer will put the rating on the foil capsule, or a label sticker or a bottle hanger. Good ratings mean good sales. Poor ones can be disastrous.

In any case, the minute the list is published, prices of the honored wines go through the roof. It's that old supply and demand thing. People want the best they can get for the least money, and if a wine appears on the list with a rating of 94 points and a price tag of $12, good luck trying to find it.

That being said, I've been following this exercise for years, and am a huge fan of buying well-considered wine for not much money. If you look carefully at the list, you'll find the values – wines that are rated 90-91 points or thereabouts, selling for under $20. There are great values (and a decent number of points) to be had for not a lot of money. You just have to spend a little time combing the list.

Drink More Wine?
We're Doing it Already.

Over in the France, Italy, and Spain, they've been making wine for literally thousands of years. Here in the US, we don't have a "wine culture" like they do, because we just haven't been doing it long enough. We also murdered our emerging wine industry during

Prohibition, and it took about half a century for American winemaking to recover just a little bit.

So other countries have always outpaced us in the amount of wine their citizens consumed and appreciated. Until now. The Wine Institute reports steady growth in wine consumption in the US over the past 15 years. In fact, it's grown by 30%, from 2 gallons per person per year in 2000 to almost 3 gallons at this writing. My "drink more wine" message must be getting through, though I certainly can't take all the credit.

Historically, the leading country in wine consumption has been France. No surprise. But wine sales in that country have been declining. Americans now consume 13% of the world's wine, and the French consume 11%. Sure, there are more people in the US than in France, but are there are other reasons why this is happening?

Partly, we can thank the Millennial generation. Even though Boomers are the largest group of wine drinkers, Millennials are gulping down an ever-increasing share – and they're coming to the wine world earlier in life. In fact, almost a third of Millennials report drinking wine on a daily basis, as opposed to less than one in five of their older counterparts. (I'm doing my part to catch up to them).

John Gillespie, President of the Wine Market Council, reports that even Gen-Xers (38-49 year olds), are "stepping up their wine consumption as they get into their middle and later thirties and early forties."

Millennials are changing the wine culture just as dramatically as they've affected the world of craft beer. First, winemakers are scrambling to create more innovative packaging, trying to attract younger consumers. One new wine called "Loco" has a cute little strait jacket around the bottle. Other packages, such as boxed and canned wine, are also growing in popularity.

Too, this generation tends to order wine by the glass in restaurants, rather than by the bottle. They're being adventurous, sampling a wider range of styles, which is affecting the way wineries produce their product. The new hotness is the wine "keg," which allows bars and restaurants to serve wine on tap, instead of from the bottle. A company called Free Flow offers the wines of over 450 well-respected wineries in kegs for on-tap service.

Where is this taking us? First, I predict that the quality of wines in boxes and cans will improve, making better beverages available in a wider variety of situations. It will be easier to take good wine along to picnics, cookouts, and similar events. Second, as demand increases, the selection of wines will expand, offering us more choice in wine styles, winegrowing regions, and even increased availability of wines made from more interesting, non-standard grape varietals.

New Year's Resolutions – You Can Make Them Any Time

I recently discovered an old column I'd saved from the *Wall Street Journal* published back in 2009, where then-wine writers Dorothy Gaiter and John Brecher made a list of 20 wine things to try in the new year. I said to myself, "Why wait?" After all, we can have wine fun whenever we darn well please. And, many of the items on their list are well worth doing at any time of year.

For example, **open a sparkling wine at home**, just because you can. So many people save Champagne and other sparkling wines for a special occasion, but you can make any dinner special by popping the cork on a bottle of fizzy. There are dozens of reasonably-priced sparkling wines on the shelves, many are Champagnes and others are made by the Champagne method. My favorite is **Gruet**, which comes from New Mexico, of all places. Their deliciously dry Brut is about $18, and worth every nickel.

Try a wine from a different country. Of course, we tend to stick to wine types and producers we've sampled and liked, but what about expanding your horizons a little? The red table wines from Portugal have become sensational values. The Portuguese have done a terrific job using the grapes traditionally vinified as Port (Touriga Nacional, Tinta Roriz, etc.) to make wines like the **Quinta das Carvalhas Touriga Nacional Douro,** with plum, cocoa, spice and currant flavors all in the bottle for around $20.

Shop at a wine store – There are many advantages to patronizing smaller shops and being advised by a merchant who's caring, knowledgeable, and really understands wine. If you try a new wine and can't find it anywhere, an independent store can special order it for you. They hold tastings and other events where you can sample different wines and expand your horizons. They can put you on preferred customer lists and give you access to wines that may not be generally available. Building a relationship with a local wine retailer in your area is always a good idea.

Splurge, for once – People who can afford to drink a $60 - $100 bottle of wine with dinner every night don't live at our house. But once in a while – not on a birthday or anniversary –go ahead and spend the money. Restaurant wine lists are often arranged by price, so start at the bottom where the "reserve" wines are, and just do it...even if it's once a year.

The Sniffing of Wine --
Or
Cats Get Frightened in Wet Months

If we know where to look, the wine we pour into our glasses can tell us all sorts of things that increase our enjoyment and appreciation. At professional tastings and evaluations, we use the previously-mentioned "Five-S" procedure to evaluate the wines in front of us. You can do it, too. And when you do, you'll have a much more complete and pleasurable experience.

The "Five-S" approach starts with "Seeing" the wine, and considering the color, brightness, and translucence. This can tell us a lot. We want the wine to be clear, bright, and brilliant. If we can see through it, we know it's going to be very light on the palate. If it's dark, we expect a bolder taste and mouthfeel. Color tells us age, as well. Red wines lose color over time, gaining a kind of brick hue. White wines gain color, turning dark yellow, then brown.

But let's focus on the second "S": the Sniff. The aromas we get "on the nose" are the biggest clue to what the wine will taste like. Sense of smell makes up about 85% of our sense of taste, so the sniffing part of the process is more important than you might think. The key is to use the letters **C-G-F-I-W-M.** You may well ask, "How the heck am I supposed to remember that?" Well, just keep in mind that Cats Get Frightened In Wet Months. Some sniffing things to consider...

Cleanliness – Does the wine smell clean and bright? Be aware of "off" aromas like cardboard or wet newspaper that might indicate the presence of "cork taint," or TCA, which robs the wine of flavor.

Grape Variety – Many grapes have distinctive aroma profiles. Do you smell cassis and dark fruits? Maybe it's a Cabernet Sauvignon. Strawberry? Could be a Pinot Noir from California.

Fruitiness – Wines can be "fruit forward," offering scents of apple, pear, pineapple, grapefruit, and tropical fruits in white wines, and red or black fruits in reds. If it's from the Old World (France, Germany, Spain, and Italy), you'll probably detect more earthy and vegetal aromas.

Intensity – Another clue to the "body" or "weight of the wine on your palate. Light aromas or big bold ones? It's a hint.

Wood – Many wines are fermented or aged in oak barrels, and some of the aromas imparted by the wood can be detected when you're a considerate sniffer. In Chardonnay, the woody sensation will be fairly obvious. In reds, you may smell more coffee, cola, chocolate, smoke, or vanilla.

Maturity – If you don't know the vintage of the wine you're drinking, your nose can give you a clue. Younger wines smell fresh and bright. Older ones have earthier aromas and fainter hints of fruit.

Of course, the real test is what happens when you proceed to the next "S": the sipping part.

Bottle Shock

Many of my wine friends have seen the movie "Bottle Shock" at least two or three times. In case you haven't, it's the true story of the blind tasting in France in 1976 that proved to the world that American wines were, for the most part, every bit as good as their famous French competitors. We referred to this in the section on winemakers.

The entire story is told in the wonderful book, *The Judgment of Paris*, by George Taber, who was a freelance writer in Paris at the time, and the only journalist interested enough to attend. Most people in France thought it was heresy to even consider that American wines might be up to their standards.

A wine store owner in Paris named Steven Spurrier set up the event. He went to Napa Valley, brought back a selection of California wines, and set up the blind tasting in a hotel ballroom in downtown Paris. (In the movie, the tasting takes place is a much more picturesque ruined stone building in the countryside).

The evaluation was performed by five or six of the
most famous, most expert wine authorities in France.
By the time they had tasted and rated all the wines,
miracle of miracles: among other highly-rated
American wines, such as Stag's Leap, Chateau
Montelena Chardonnay from Napa Valley came in
first. The French were incredulous. Mortified. Very
upset. Their evaluation, proving that an American
wine can be equal in quality and sophistication to the
finest, most expensive white Burgundies, shook the
foundations of the international wine trade. Seriously.
The American reds did even better. In fact, there is a
bottle of the Chateau Montelena 1973 Chardonnay on
display in the Smith-sonian. That's how important the
event was.

What the movie does not mention is that the
Montelena Chardonnay was not made by the winery's
owner Jim Barrett or by his son Bo, both of whom are
the central focus of the picture. It was, in fact, made
by their winemaker, a young Croatian immigrant
named Mike Grgich. It is said that he's not depicted in
the film because he didn't want to be involved. So the
Barretts are front and center, and Mike has about 10
seconds of screen time, if you know exactly where to
look.

Shortly after the Judgment of Paris put Chateau
Montelena and other Napa wines on the world map,
Grgich set out on his own, establishing his Grgich
Hills winery in 1976. He's been turning out great juice
every year since. You may have already discovered
him in Part III of this book.

Can You Can Wine?

As a wine writer, I receive samples from wineries and their public relations firms. Some of them have come in cans. Upon reflection, I concluded that wine can reasonably be stored in any kind of non-reactive container, even a can. In fact, I've seen wines that come in cute plastic individual wine tumblers with a stem and everything. So there's really no good reason, aside from tradition and maybe a bit of snobbishness, that wine can't be placed in a convenient, airtight can. It works for beer.

The issue, however, is not the preservation of the beverage, but the quality. These days, winemakers are appealing strongly to Millennials by developing cutesy names and packages for all kinds of wine. Previously, I noted the new "Loco" wines from Spain that come wrapped in an adorable little strait jacket. A bit extreme, perhaps, but they do get attention.

The market for canned wine more than doubled as I was preparing this book for publication, and amounted to over $6 million in sales. A drop in the wine bucket compared to the overall industry, but a fivefold increase over 2012. As we know, cans are especially efficient at containing bubbly beverages, so it's no surprise that most of the increase came from sparkling wines like mini-Champagnes, and easy-drinking casual wines, such as rosé.

Recent consumer surveys stress the desirability of keeping the wine at the proper temperature and being able to take it just about anywhere. So there's quite a bit to be said for packaging wine this way. You can take it all kinds of places without having to lug heavy bottles or large ice chests. But the big question, of course, is this: is the stuff any good?

The answer is a qualified yes. Most of us are not going to take a $200 bottle to the beach or the parking lot outside the stadium, so the quality of most canned wines is in the middle range, which is okay.

What Goes With What?

Wine lovers, whether beginning or advanced, are always confronted with new things to learn. Wines from unheard-of regions suddenly appear on the shelves (anybody know where Yecla is?), a new type of grape, once thought extinct, is now being vinified and bottled. (So if you have any Piculit Neri in your cellar, be sure to let me know).

But perhaps one of the biggest challenges for all of us is trying to pair up wines with different types of food. There are, of course, combinations that are known as "classic pairings": Port with Stilton cheese, for example, and foie gras with Sauternes. Less elevated combinations include one we all know and love: Chianti with red sauce dishes like pasta and pizza. Beyond that, things get a bit sticky.

Part of the puzzle is trying to find pairings for popular dishes that come from non-wine cultures, like China, India, and Thailand. There are solutions, and some great pairings, but that's a chapter all by itself.

Mostly, it's a matter of food chemistry. Why does no wine in the world go with asparagus or artichokes? What acids and other flavor components in a particular dish will enhance (or fight with) the chemistry of the food? A good example is citric acid, which is very predominant in wines like Sauvignon Blanc, especially the New Zealand versions. That leads to the previously mentioned "the lemon law." If you can put lemon on a dish, you can drink Sauvignon Blanc with it.

Here's another: if you're drinking a very tannic young red wine, pair it with a salty food. At a professional tasting a few years ago, we sipped a young tannic wine, which puckered us up pretty well. Then we had a lick of salt and tasted the wine again. No tannins. Works with walnuts, too.

There are other aids and little tricks available. The Internet is full of "food pairing charts" that try to communicate the information graphically. Some are simple diagrams, and others are poster-sized tables with hundreds of listings and combinations.

Many times, wine and food pairings surprise us. For example, we paired grilled sea scallops with Chardonnay, when we'd normally go right for the Sauvignon Blanc. Many Chardonnays are made with a slant toward acidity rather than the typical buttery flavor profile. Acidity is a perfect balance to the texture of the dish, especially when there are notes of lemon zest and minerality which accent the lemon in the dish. A typical example of the "lemon law."

Pork belly and Riesling? Instinct tells us that this type of meat demands a big red. However, a dry Riesling will have the acidity to cut through and neutralize the fattiness of the pork belly. Unusual, but very interesting.

Third, try an earthy Pinot Noir with duck breast confit. A Burgundy would probably be best. The earthiness of the Pinot supports the smoky character of the broiled duck, each one enhancing the other.

While it's not possible to list every dish that goes with every wine, there are some basic principles that you can apply to almost every situation.

1] ***Champagne goes with anything***. Same with other sparkling whites made in the Champagne method. We drink it at Thanksgiving because it works with all the different sweet and salty flavors of the different dishes.

2] ***Old world wines go with old world foods***. They've evolved together for centuries. Don't fight tradition. A Chianti Classico with (maybe) pasta and veal ragú would be sensational.

3] ***Sweet and spicy barbecue sauces need bold, fruity wines***, like Zinfandel...or Malbec from Argentina.

4] ***Cabernet Sauvignon is heaven with grilled meat dishes***. And, as we all know, that's why the regional flag of the Margaux region in Bordeaux has a sheep on it.

For more information, go to Google Images and type in "Food and Wine Pairing." You'll be overwhelmed at the number of charts, graphs, and diagrams.

Global Warming –
Good News For Wine Lovers?

Whether or not you accept the science behind global warming studies, it's a fact that weather has a huge role to play in the quality of the wines we enjoy. For example, in the last few years the Bordeaux region in France has experienced warmer-than-usual summers. The result: excellent vintages, because of the increase in sunlight.

According to an article by Benjamin Plackett in *USA Today,* winemakers in the region are predicting that the 2015 vintage will be "historic," and that the wines will be able to stay in the cellar, gaining quality, for up to 30 years. I won't be buying any, unless I want to leave them to my grandchildren.

In Bordeaux, as well as in other winegrowing regions, quality has been on the rise because growing seasons have become progressively warmer, yielding riper grapes with higher concentrations of sugar and other critical flavor and structural components. Also, the increase in temperatures allows for an earlier harvest, often in September instead of October. What's the difference? It starts raining in October, and the last thing growers want is rain during harvest: the grapes take up the water, diluting the strength and quality of the juice, and making the wine weaker and less palatable. Picking in drier September – if the grapes are ripe enough – avoids that serious problem.

Agencies that measure this sort of thing report that average temperatures in France have risen by a bit more than half a degree per decade since 1960. That means summers are now about 2.5 degrees warmer than they used to be. It doesn't sound like a lot, but it's a big deal when you're a grape.

Plackett's article reports that many French winemakers are convinced warmer summers have been beneficial to the harvests. Beatrice Laurensan from Château la Gaffilière is quoted as saying "The term 'bad vintage' is gone."

The news, however, is not all good. Looking to the future, continued rising temperatures and less rainfall mean that good vintages may well become less frequent. France's southerly wine regions, which are closer to the Mediterranean, are already reporting water stress due to lack of rain.

Studies during the last few years by the National Academy of Sciences indicate that rising temperatures will force winemakers to make some adjustments in their techniques...even forcing them to move vineyards to higher ground, where temperatures are cooler. And the correlation between higher heat and lower rainfall doesn't hold true everywhere. While this phenomenon might be beneficial (at least in the short term) in Bordeaux and Burgundy, it could easily have the opposite effect in California. The region frequently experiences enormous flooding in winegrowing regions that may well be just the beginning.

As with most global trends, only time will tell. For now, however, the Bordelais, Burgundians, and their compatriots in Champagne and the Rhône are enjoying all that summer sunshine.

Natural Wines – The Next Big Thing

There's a reason why so-called "natural" wines are making such a big impression these days. Mostly, it's an indication of the overall trend for foods and lifestyles that are closer to the earth. Non-GMO products, all-natural ingredients, yoga, and the like.

In Naples, Florida, one resident is betting the farm (so to speak) on the quality and appeal of natural wines. He's Peter Rizzo, and his new store, Natural Wines Naples, is educating both wine lovers and newbies to the flavors and appeal of natural wines. In other parts of the country, some wine store owners are doing the same thing.

More about Peter in a second, but first let's figure out what natural wines really are. Basically, they're made in the purest, simplest way possible. Vineyards are organic or even biodynamic. Winemakers use only naturally-occurring yeasts to induce fermentation – no addition of other yeast strains.

Plus, the winemaking is what's known as "non-interventionist." That means no filtering, no additives, no manipulation. Grow the grapes, crush them, and let nature take its course.

"These wines have a place on every wine lover's shelf," says Peter Rizzo. "They're very expressive, and a lot more interesting than wines made in a more commercial manner. I really believe in this." And so do I, after the tasting session we shared.

Even though natural wines are uncharted territory for most of us, there are plenty of reasons to get to know them. These winemakers believe that great wine is made in the vineyard. The growing areas are free from any insecticides, pesticides, herbicides or other chemicals. The wines are made without any additives, no extra acid or flavoring compounds, no industrial yeasts or enzymes, and extremely minimal sulfur content. There's no weird manipulation, like micro-oxygenation, reverse osmosis, or concentrators. As you might expect, vineyard yields are low, so quantities are not very high.

The result: wines that are alive, that express a sense of place, and that improve – quickly – over time.

Rizzo, who spent most of his career in advertising, relocated with his family to Naples in 2002 and opened Natural Wines Naples in October of 2016. Since then, he's seen a steady increase in interest, and in store traffic. While some natural wines are made from fairly exotic out-of-the-way varietals (I saw a bottle of Romortin and Orbois blend), you'd recognize the vast majority of wines in his selection.

"I need to show people classic representations," he believes. "Even though many makers of natural wines push the envelope with non-traditional varietals, we have all the classic wines, and all the classic flavors. Just because a wine is natural, it doesn't sacrifice the familiar taste profiles we all enjoy."

He makes sure of that, with extensive descriptions of each wine's flavor and aroma profiles on bottle tags that he hand-writes. And he's especially proud of the fact that his wine selection offers interesting choices in all price ranges.

"There's nothing rare or exotic about natural wines," says Rizzo. "You might be surprised to see some bottles with crown caps on them instead of corks, and we do have some wines made from grapes you may not be familiar with, but natural wines include all your favorites, and many of them are priced under $20."

Doing What Comes Naturally

In the previous section, I introduced a relatively new phenomenon (or trend) in the wine world: natural wines. The piece profiled Peter Rizzo, who operates a wine store in Southwest Florida that specializes in nothing but wines that are made in the most "natural" way. Much to my surprise, delight, and personal vindication, just after I met Rizzo, *Wine Spectator* magazine devoted quite a bit of ink to exactly this issue, but specifically as it relates to how natural wines are becoming more widely accepted (and purchased) in France.

As we all know, France is what you might call the "mistress of wine." Most of the wines we enjoy have French names. Cabernet Sauvignon. Sauvignon Blanc. Chardonnay. So when the French start making a fuss about natural wines, we might want to pay attention.

In an article entitled "France Tries to Define Natural Wine," writer Susan Mustachich observes that wine bars in Paris that carry only natural wines have "proliferated," and this type of wine has been enthusiastically adopted by young professionals, Millennials, and other major wine consumers.

The problem is this: there is no legal definition of natural wine, neither in France nor the US. So what – exactly – are we talking about here?

In France, the growing, production, and sale of wine are controlled by a government bureau known as the INAO. Right now they're trying to sort out the terminology that denotes "organic" wine versus the words that are being used for "natural" wine. No easy task.

We don't have anything like the INAO in the US. Here, the trade is governed by the Bureau of Alcohol, Tobacco, and Firearms, which gives me the giggles every time I think about it. But the INAO is a powerful agency, and according to *Wine Spectator,* they've more or less agreed that "natural" wines must be made from grapes grown organically or biodynamically, that they're made only with indigenous yeast, and that winemakers make no adjustments to acidity or sugar levels. Plus, the grapes must be picked by hand.

However, natural winemakers themselves can't agree on the rules. The article reports that they avoid adding sulfites, a preservative that helps keep the wine from spoiling. Others say they do add some, but only in "difficult years." And what's more, the INAO can't define any way to judge whether one winemaking process is any more or less "natural" than any other.

So if the French, who have been doing the wine thing for thousands of years, can't figure it out, what chance have we got?

The solution – if there is one – seems to be the standards and processes cited in the previous section, and supported by Peter Rizzo and other natural wine proponents. Natural wine is (more or less) organic wine with no additives and no external manipulation.

Then the question is, how much difference does it actually make? People sensitive to sulfites, histamines, and other normal wine components might be better off seeking out natural wines. And certainly, a direct and "non-interventionist" approach to winemaking can't be a bad thing.

Meanwhile, allow me to suggest that we all sample natural wines alongside our other favorites. They may be naturally pleasing, and well worth a try.

The Wines of the Cult

If you spend any time hanging around wine aficionados, or read anything on the subject, you might come across a mention of California's so-called "cult wines." No, these are not the wines you drink while waiting for the mother ship to take you back to your home planet, nor do you carry them when you trek deep into the jungle in Guyana en route to your communal living experience with Daddy.

There are five, maybe six cult wines among the top California names, and they're held in worshipful awe by a worldwide community of enthusiasts. Why? Well, they are of stunning quality, of course, but there are hundreds of equally stunning wines in the world, and they cost just as much. These particular brands are cult wines mostly because you can't get any.

In no particular order, most people agree that the major wines are Screaming Eagle, Harlan Estate, Grace Family, Bryant Family, Marcassin, Hundred

Acre, and one or two others. Mention these names
and your wine friends will get a yummy look on their
faces.

Maybe it's just a question of rarity. After all, the most
famous wines of Bordeaux sell for upwards of $750 a
bottle, but each chateau makes around 18,000 cases
of the stuff every year. Harlan Estate has only 36
acres under vine, and at this level the goal is not to
grow the most grapes, it's to grow the fewest.
Overproduction weakens the wine, so winemakers
prune bunches off the vines (crying as they cut) to
concentrate more flavor in fewer grapes. Screaming
Eagle makes maybe 500 three-bottle cases a year, and
if you're lucky enough to be on their allocation list,
they'll sell you just one three-pack for around $2,500.
Private collectors and amusingly expensive
restaurants all want some, so demand is, to put it
mildly, frenzied and desperate.

Okay. Cult wines are expensive, and they're very
limited in production. Is that where the mystique
comes from? Not exactly. There are other producers in
the world who make wine in ridiculously small
quantities. In Burgundy, a producer may own only five
or six rows of vines in a particular vineyard, and will
make a few hundred bottles, if that. Some of them
cost more than a mortgage payment.

Myths and legends arise from the popular culture. In
this case, cult status is bestowed by serious wine lifers
who got themselves on the allocation list 20 years ago,
and hedge fund managers who buy them on the
secondary market. Example: a three-bottle case of
Screaming Eagle 2012 costs mailing list members

$2,250. It generally sells for $6,000 at auction – or more.

We've been fortunate enough to sample many of these wines, and they're indeed extraordinary. But life-changing? Fortunately, they're all available through online retailers or auction sites, so you can actually try them. When you do, ask yourself one question: are they worth upwards of $750 a bottle? We'll let your own taste – and credit limit – decide that one.

Wine From the Old World... Not the Old Country

One of the things I like best about wine appreciation is that you can learn about it by dividing the wine world in half. Reds and whites. Old World and New World. But it's that "Old World" distinction that makes a lot of aspiring wine lovers take a step back. Truth is, the "New World" wines are a lot easier to get your arms around, because they put the name of the grape right there on the label. Cabernet Sauvignon. Chardonnay. Deciphering the wines from places like France, Spain, Italy, and Germany requires a bit more work, but not that much. And the effort is worth it.

As I stated previously, they've been making wine over there for thousands of years. France, for example, is known as "the mistress of wine," and every aspiring winemaker has to make a basic choice right from the start. Do I make my wine in the French style, or not?

What makes this whole thing a bit complicated (and fun) is that the vast majority of Old World wines don't carry the name of the grape on the label. They tell you where it's from, instead, because that's what they care about over there. You look at the label, and it says Chianti, or Barolo, or Chinon, or Sancerre. So what the heck are we drinking?

I've been wrestling with how to make this as easy as possible, because, quite honestly, figuring out Old World wines is something of a challenge, and it's why people read wine books and go to tastings. Luckily, even though there are hundreds of grapes used in winemaking, we don't have to worry about most of them.

We might as well start with the reds. In many places, wines are made from different grapes blended together, because each variety adds its own quality to the final mix. One wine might be included for structure, another for color, and a third gets thrown in for aroma. So if you like red Bordeaux, you're most likely drinking a blend of Cabernet Sauvignon, Merlot, Petit Verdot, Cabernet Franc, and maybe a little Malbec.

If the bottle is a red from the northern Rhône, you'll be enjoying mostly Syrah. In the southern Rhône, around Châteauneuf du Pape, things get messy. Most reds from this area are a blend of Syrah, Grenache, and Mourvèdre, but the law allows winemakers to blend in as many as thirteen grapes, and five of them are white. Go figure.

In one way (and only in one way) Burgundy is the easiest. If you have a glass of red Burgundy in front of you, you're drinking Pinot Noir. If it's white, it's Chardonnay. That's it. Problem is that there are 707 distinct regions in Burgundy, and the wines from each of them are different. It's harder to understand than Chinese algebra, so have fun.

Then there's the Loire Valley, one of my favorite places because if the label says Chinon or Bourgueil, there's Cabernet Franc in the bottle. It's a big, bold red wine, with lots of structure and flavor...great with steaks and heartily sauced meat dishes.

What's left? Of course...Champagne. In this small area about 90 miles northeast of Paris, they make the world's most famous bubbly from Chardonnay, Pinot Noir, and a grape called Pinot Meuniere. Weird thing is, most Champagnes are white, but two of the three grapes used in the blend are red. The red grapes are carefully crushed, and the juice drained off before it has a chance to pick up any color from the skins. Then, the winemaker might blend together wines made from as many as 50 different vineyards to arrive at the final "house style." A labor of love, to be sure.

As you can imagine, they make wine all over the Old World, so the best advice is this. Be adventurous. Find a wine store with people who really know their wines and can help you. And sample widely.

What's In YOUR Wine?

The question always arises: is wine simply the result of crushing grapes and letting the juice ferment, or is anything added to wine to improve quality or cover up flaws? The answer is mostly yes. At least for lower-end products.

As I've mentioned many times, there is no consumer product in the world that give you less information about what's in the package than a wine label. But some few winemakers steadfastly maintain a "non-interventionist" approach, adding nothing or very little to the wine, and they actually list ingredients on the bottle. This, however, is extremely rare.

On the other hand, makers of very inexpensive wines, like the stuff that comes in three-liter boxes with a little plastic faucet on the side, have a lot at stake because they make wine in industrial quantities. Since they're cooking the stuff up 300,000 gallons at a time they have to (a) save money, (b) assure uniformity and (c) make sure nothing goes wrong in the process. These producers use several techniques (and several substances) to maximize production and minimize risk.

First, there's sugar. If there's not enough residual sugar in the juice, the yeast won't be able to convert it into sufficient alcohol. Winemakers add beet or cane sugar (a process called chaptalization) to increase alcohol content. It doesn't make the wine sweeter, because it's consumed during fermentation. This is illegal in most countries, but a common practice in Germany and some other places.

Then, there's oak, which adds all sorts of flavors and dimensions to wine. If you can't afford barrels, which cost upwards of $1,500 each, you throw planks of oak into the juice. If you can't afford them, you use oak chips. And if you're really on a budget, you use oak sawdust, then filter it out before bottling.

Next is vitamins, which keep yeast alive in the juice during fermentation. These may be added in high-alcohol wines (over about 14%).

Acid content (pH) is extremely important to overall taste and balance. If acid levels are too high or low, substances can be used to make the adjustment. Too little acid might call for the addition of tartaric, malic, or citric acid. These are very common ingredients in many of the foods we eat, and are not at all harmful.

Tannins occur naturally in grape skins and seeds and are the critical structural component of red wine. If there's not enough, powdered tannin can be used to add muscle to an otherwise weak wine.

Now it's time to talk about Rubired grapes. As the name implies, they're really really red and are used to make a concentrate called Mega Purple. This can be added to red wines to boost the color and make the wine look consistent from batch to batch. In California, in 2013, over 255,000 tons of these grapes were harvested. Winemakers won't admit on the record to using it, but the word is that even makers of more expensive wines drop some in to deepen the color. Since it's basically grape juice, it's not considered an additive.

There are other processes which don't involve putting substances in the wine, but are also used to improve quality. Micro-oxygenation blows tiny air bubbles into the juice to open up and smooth out tannins. Reverse osmosis forces the liquid through a membrane to filter out impurities and increase flavor concentration.

All that being said, there's no reason to fear opening your favorite bottle. These substances don't remain in the wine: they're used in miniscule amounts to eliminate flaws, then completely removed. And besides, they're also naturally present in many of the foods we eat. So keep swirling and sipping!

Wines and Valentines
-- or --
Candy is Dandy, but Liquor is Quicker

It happens every year, right around middle to late January. Wineries and their PR firms send me samples of wines that are "perfect" for the "romantic" Valentine's holiday. Their accompanying emails say things like "encourage your readers to let Italy's Chianti region inspire a boost in romance," or "Prosecco is an affordable luxury for that candle-lit dinner," or "try this new rosé offering for Valentine's Day."

What's more, for some reason most of the purveyors want us to believe that if we truly desire to create a romantic mood, the wine should have bubbles. Now, I'm a firm believer that one shouldn't wait for a so-called "special occasion" to open a bottle of Champagne or other sparkling wine. After all, Champagne is (mostly) Chardonnay with bubbles in it, and goes perfectly with an enormous range of foods...so why wait until your team wins the big game, or that job promotion comes through?

And yet...practically every day in late December and early January, we columnists receive boxes of wine samples (especially bubblies) urging us to present them to you as the way to your loved one's heart.

Maybe they're right. After all, most of us have a strong, if subconscious, association with the idea that sparkling wines are for special occasions and celebrations. We see it in the movies all the time. In "The Italian Job," Mark Wahlberg, Donald Sutherland, and their accomplices steal a ton of money and survive a frantic boat chase through the canals of Venice, then celebrate on a snowy mountaintop by swigging Dom Perignon straight from the bottle. And who hasn't witnessed elated members of a victorious sports team drenching each other with bubbly in the locker room after they clinch the trophy?

Then, of course, there's the expense. Champagne (the real stuff, from the legally-designated Champagne region of France) is created through a laborious and complex process that involves blending up to 50 wines from different vineyards, inducing secondary fermentation in the bottle, disgorging the dead yeast cells, and lots more. That's expensive. There are, of course, both true Champagnes and other types of festive sparkling wines that are more value priced for your Valentine's Day celebration. It's nice to spend $350 on a bottle of Salon or Dom, but you can get into a romantic mood just as easily with a great tasting wine at a tenth of the price. So let's do that. Pour a few glasses, and love one another.

PART V
WOMEN AND WINE

oys and girls are different. So one of the topics that gets brought up continually in the wine world is how men and women approach, discuss, and experience wine. As if the subject of wine weren't interesting enough...

For some reason I keep coming back to this topic and have often written about the fascinating differences between the sexes as they enjoy the wine experience. This is true for travel, tasting, glassware, all aspects of this pleasurable and educational pursuit.

I'm not the only one. As I mention in the following chapter, there are millions of ways women participate as winemakers and marketers, in the restaurant industry, as consumers. There are dozens, if not hundreds, of books and articles ruminating on this very topic. And the ways women diverge from men in tasting and discussing are probably worth a book all by itself.

Women and Wine. And Women.

It wasn't all that long ago. You asked for the wine list in a restaurant and the server automatically handed it to the man at the table. For many reasons, wine has traditionally been thought of as a guy thing. Not anymore.

In the past, of course, most (if not all) winemaking operations were under the control of the male of the species. In Burgundy, for example, before Napoleon came along and straightened everyone out, vineyard properties were always left to the first-born male. But over the past 30-40 years or so we've seen a shift. First, many female winemakers, like Helen Turley, Pam Starr, and Heidi Barrett in the US, have made a significant impact by making important (and expensive, highly-rated) wines. And since winemaking is traditionally a family business, many winemakers have brought their daughters into major roles in both the production and marketing sides of the operation.

In Italy, top-level winemakers Angelo Gaja and Piero Antinori have both ceded a good deal of responsibility to their daughters. In the US, Tim Mondavi's daughter Carissa plays a major role at their Continuum winery. The same thing is happening in other parts of the world.

But France has always taken the lead in giving these opportunities to women. As far back as 1805, Champagne maker François Cliquot died and left his winery to his wife, Barbe-Nicole Ponsardin. The widow (*veuve* in French) Cliquot built the company into the iconic enterprise it is today. And several major wineries in Bordeaux, such as Chateau Margaux and Chateau Lanessan, have prospered under the direction of female owners.

But what is even more interesting is that in today's wine trade, women who anchor winemaking families devote themselves to not only making and marketing wine, but to forming groups for "discussing moderate wine consumption" and "its benefits in a healthy lifestyle." They call themselves "Women For WineSense," and, as members of the wine-trade, work toward getting balanced consumer information placed on wine labels. Several of the members' names appear on those very bottles: Margaret Duckhorn, Rosemary Cakebread, Annette Shafer, Susan Sokol-Blosser, Cathy Clifton, Margrit Mondavi, and many more.

Some women make wine, some sell it. While the traditional image of a restaurant sommelier is almost exclusively masculine, the number of female somms has gone through the roof. Restaurant groups like Danny Meyer's Union Square Hospitality Group have several women in positions that are critical both for guest relations and wine sales.

As noted above, more and more women are making wine decisions...and that includes at the restaurant table. Kristene Hansen noted in a blog on the subject that women who dine out may feel more comfortable and less intimidated discussing wine with a female sommelier. Hansen discovered another interesting point: men often order a pricier wine from a woman than they would from a man.

But even more interesting is the way women think of wine, purchase it, and drink it. Vinexpo, the worldwide trade marketing organization, researches this sort of thing, and the trends are very revealing.

These female behaviors are probably the result of certain fundamental differences in gender nature and nurture. It has long been proposed that women perceive and actually taste things (especially wine) differently than their male counterparts. There may be actual reasons for that, involving basic physiology and body chemistry. French wine critic Isabel Forêt has written extensively about just this phenomenon in her annual "guide to wine for women." Subtitled "How to Love and Understand Wine," it runs to over 500 pages. She notes that, of every five bottles of wine that are purchased in France, three are bought by women. Also, she draws a clear distinction between the "character" of wines that appeal to men in contrast with those that women are more likely to enjoy. Specifically, she says that women's wines are generally more fruit-forward, more refined and "supple," with lower levels of tannin.

That may be true. According to Forêt, and in my (admittedly anecdotal) experience, women not only perceive and taste wine differently (as mentioned above), they approach the wine world with different attitudes and goals. In the introduction to her book, Forêt says, "women are more sensual, their breathing is different...they perceive aromas more subjectively. Wine is more than just a simple beverage, it is a combination of aromas that open in the mouth, offering an infinite number of sensations." Women, she says have more olfactory sensitivity to perfumes, to the aromas of foods, to the scents of the home. These differences are supported by studies done by geneticists, biologists, neurologists, and even sex researchers.

True. Women direct their attention and their interest to the hedonistic side of wine consumption, focusing on the flavors, aromas, and sensual aspects. Men, on the other hand, concentrate more on the grape varietal, soil type, where the wine was made...the factual stuff.

Plus, women think about and perceive wine in different ways. The vast majority of women believe that drinking wine is compatible with maintaining a healthy, balanced diet: this is particularly true in the US. They also see it as an enhancement of special social events and fine food. Vinexpo research shows that older women enjoy wine more. Over 70% of women 60+ say they drink at least one glass per week, compared to 60% of 18-to-30 year olds.

It's a common belief that women prefer white wines, but research tells a different story. The split is actually

60-40 in favor of reds. And when they buy wine, they don't depend on male advice or assistance. Over 60% of women in the US make their own choices.

And more recently, especially with the development of social media, there are hundreds of women's wine clubs, tasting groups, business and social networks.

As I was preparing this chapter, an organization called "Women and Wine on Wednesdays" had chapters in 13 cities, and was seeking to expand to many others. The site asks women who join to "come enjoy a glass of wine and take advantage of this unique opportunity to catch up with old friends and to meet some new ones – to exchange ideas, share resources, discover new opportunities in a comfortable and welcome atmosphere." The founding principle seems to be that wine is a gateway to social and personal relationships. The site says, "for centuries, wine has proven to liven the senses, cause thoughts to flow, and enhance friendly idea exchanges - so wine is a perfect accompaniment, blending to foster a relaxed and welcoming environment for sharing resources, idea exchanges, and a great reason to take time for yourself." Many other women's web-based groups seem to follow similar principles.

In fact, female members of the international wine club Direct Cellars spontaneously formed their own sub-group within the organization and called themselves "The Women of DC." They have a separate Facebook page, and interact with each other apart from the club's many thousands of members.

However, in reading through the About Us on these sites, it seems as though the purpose of women gathering to share a glass or three doesn't have much to do with the wine. Most sites promote the social and comfort aspects, the meeting new people, networking, sharing, exchanging. Again, in my anecdotal experience, when men gather to open a few bottles, all they talk about is what's in the glass. They deconstruct the flavor profile, relate what happened the last time they visited that particular winery, argue about soil composition, try to remember how much they paid. Women seem to talk about anything but.

The relationship between women and wine is reflected in movies and television dramas, as well. There are more series than ever that feature wine-loving women in leading roles, such as "The Good Wife," or Connie Britton's character in "Friday Night Lights." Wine also is a part of the lives of women such as Skyler White in "Breaking Bad," and Claire Danes' character on "Homeland." That's much different than the Cosmos that were so enthusiastically consumed by Carrie Bradshaw and her crew on "Sex and the City."

In a *Huffington Post* article, writer Emma Gray observes that for her, wine has always been a "means for connection and relaxation." It's a female ritual that has been promoted (maybe "propounded" is a better word) by popular culture. Gray cites Maya Rudolph's and Kristin Wiig's magazine and wine party in "Bridesmaids," as well as the guzzling cast of "Cougar Town."

As it happens, there's a commercial side to the combination of women, wine, and social relationships. It's probably no surprise that many companies tap into it as a way of selling products and services.

One such is Five Rings Financial, an investment brokerage based in Colorado. They call their approach "Women, Wine, and Wealth." Notice the order of the words. They invite women to join a wine social club where they can "network with other women in your area, share laughs over good wine and [just by coincidence] learn about the information you need to make better financial decisions." Other companies may soon follow suit.

So here are some suggestions for your next white tablecloth dining experience. First, don't be surprised when your sommelier is a well-educated, well-traveled woman who knows the wine world from top to bottom. Second, servers have learned to not automatically offer the wine list to the man at the table. There's an excellent chance that a discriminating and wine-savvy woman will be making the selection.

The French Pronounce it "Terr-WAH"

Terroir. It's a word from the wine world, and like most of them, it's French. And like most French words, it means more than just the limited definition of "earth" or "land" or "dirt."

In winespeak, "terroir" refers to the specific place where the grapes are grown. But, as mentioned above, it's much more than that. In the widest sense, it means *everything* about that specific place: the soil, elevation, drainage, the direction the vineyard faces, how the fog from the ocean keeps the grapes cool in the morning, and what time it burns off. And in a way, even the winemaking traditions of the particular area.

In many regions, the soil is very site-specific. My vineyard may have a vein of limestone running beneath it, which imparts certain qualities to the grapes grown there. My neighbor's vineyard, just a few feet on the other side of the cart path, doesn't have any limestone. That's why I get $5,000 a ton for my grapes, and he has to sell his for only $2,000.

The concept of terroir varies in importance and significance depending on the country and region. In the Old World (France, Spain, Italy, Germany) it's critical. Grapes grown in a certain region, vineyard, and even a particular part of a vineyard are carefully – and precisely -- classified. In fact, wine is the very first product in history to establish and promote geographic indications. We don't do it with broccoli or asparagus.

But there's some indication that the idea of giving winegrowing regions specific geographical indications is more of a marketing ploy than a designation of quality. According to a recent article in *Forbes* magazine, this whole idea of a link between location and quality is a big sticking point in international trade disputes. The question is, should we, as wine lovers, care about this? Well...yes.

As far back as 1756, in Portugal, wealthy vineyard owners lobbied for special designations of quality...for their own properties, of course. From this, regulations were established about which grapes could be grown where, and other laws about how the wine must be made. Today, it's much more complex than that.

In Europe, and especially in France, there are government ministries, like wine police, that decree which vineyards are in the "St. Julien" appellation, for example, and why the vineyards 100 feet away across the cart path aren't. And these decrees are strictly enforced. In the US, the delineation of American Viticultural Areas (AVAs) is controlled by the Bureau of Alcohol, Tobacco, and Firearms. I've mentioned previously how amusing this is to me.

Nevertheless, knowing where your wine comes from can be important. Certain grapes grow best in certain areas, and it makes a difference (especially in the price) whether your Cabernet Sauvignon comes from Napa or Noplace. It's the climate, the fog off the river or ocean, the kind of yeast that grows on the grapes...it's everything.

All the Wine Wisdom You Need to Flabbergast Your Friends, Astound Your Associates, Amaze Your Acquaintances, and Dumbfound Your Dates.

PART VI
ASK THE WINE WHISPERER

F didn't include any questions I don't know the answers to.

*As Wine Director of an international wine club, I receive
many emails from members with questions about wine.
In this section, I've compiled a group of inquiries that
deal with general wine topics, and are submitted to me
quite frequently. They're in no particular order, but I
hope they help to answer some questions you might
have had.*

What's the proper temperature for serving wine?

When served too cold, a wine "shuts down," and the
flavors and aromas become muted. However, the
guidelines vary for different types of wine. Sparkling
wines should be served ice cold, between 40 and 50
degrees. Whites are best around 55 degrees (which is
cellar temperature), and reds at about 62 – not room
temperature. If you put a bottle of red in the
refrigerator for about 30 minutes, the serving
temperature should be ideal.

I've seen the word "Meritage" on red wine labels. Is it just a blend or is there something special about it?

First of all, when a winemaker puts the word
"Meritage" (rhymes with "heritage") on the label, it's
not just a blend of any old red wines. There is actually
a Meritage association, formed in 1988, and the term
is licensed to member wineries. The "meritage"
designation indicates that the wine is a blend of at
least two of classic varietals found in Bordeaux wines:
Cabernet Sauvignon, Merlot, Cabernet Franc, Malbec,
and Petite Verdot. Sometimes the back label will tell
you that, and sometimes not.

How many grapes does it take to make a bottle of wine?

We call this wine math. An acre of vineyard can produce anywhere from two to thirteen tons of grapes, depending on how severely the grower limits the yield. The fewer tons, the better the wine. Let's assume that a grower produces five tons of grapes per acre. That works out to about 13.5 barrels, or just under 4,000 bottles. A single bottle holds just about four glasses, unless you're using those really big wine glasses...like we do.

I've heard that grapevines get wiped out by a disease called phylloxera. What is it?

Phylloxera isn't a disease – it's an insect. Specifically, a microscopic louse that infests the roots of grapevines and kills them. When it first struck Europe and the rest of the world in the 19th Century, nobody could figure out why the vines were dying in droves, because the bug is so small as to be nearly invisible. It turns out that American rootstock is very resistant, so European vineyards were completely uprooted and replanted with the American variety. Then, winegrowers grafted the European varietals on American rootstock. The phylloxera louse is still a problem, but at least now winegrowers know what to look for and how to deal with it.

I'm concerned about calorie content. Is wine fattening?

There are between 80 to 100 calories in a four-ounce glass of wine. Sweeter wines have more carbohydrates because of the residual sugar content. If you want to reduce calories, try lighter whites, such as Sauvignon Blanc. Wine contains no fat or cholesterol.

I had this great bottle at a restaurant and would like to buy more. What's the best way to find it?

I always start in my local wine stores. Many times, a good local wine merchant can look up the distributor and help you find the wine. If that doesn't work, try wine-searcher.com, wineaccess.com, and winezap.com. Chances are one of those sites will list a retailer you can order from and have the wine shipped to you.

My local wine store has so many bottles under $15. If a wine is not expensive, does that mean it's not good quality?

Many times, the price of a wine and its quality are way out of whack. There are plenty of highly-rated wines that sell for under $15-$20 a bottle. Don't be hesitant to sample an inexpensive wine. Try one bottle. If you like it, go back and get some more.

What is blanc de blanc Champagne?

Sparkling white wine made according to the traditional Champagne method is generally a blend of three different varietals: Chardonnay, Pinot Noir, and Pinot Meuniere. A blanc de blanc ('white of whites") is made from Chardonnay only.

What are 'legs' in wine, and what do they indicate?

There's a common misunderstanding that "legs," or the rivulets of wine that run down the inside of the glass when you swirl, are an indication of quality. In fact, winemakers have been known to add glycerin to their wines to make legs for that very reason. Actually, legs are caused by the difference in evaporation rates between water and alcohol. So if legs tell you anything, they're a rough indication of the alcohol content in the wine...not the quality.

What is meant by "malolactic fermentation"?
Wines contain many types of acids. Two of the major ones are malic acid, which is found in apples, and lactic acid, which should sound familiar because it's in butter, milk, and other dairy products. Malolactic fermentation is a process initiated by the winemaker to convert some or all of the malic acid in wine to lactic acid. Depending on how long the winemaker allows the process to go on, it tones down zingy, acidic qualities, and results in a wine that's fuller on the palate, and, in whites, imparts unctuous "buttery" qualities. Strictly speaking, malolactic is not fermentation at all. It's the conversion of one type of acid to another.

How important is the vintage of a wine?
Vintage, the year shown on the bottle of most fine wines, reflects the year in which the grapes were picked. This is important because wine grapes are an agricultural product, and weather conditions can have a significant effect on the wine.

The more expensive the wine, the more important the vintage. Everyday wines (in the $10-$15 range) are made from grapes that come from several vineyards over a wide area. (For example, if the label on a bottle says "California," the grapes can come from anywhere in the state). If the harvest is not so good in one place during a particular year, the producer will find better fruit somewhere else. But if you're buying wine from very specific regions or vineyards, it's worth looking up the quality of that year's harvest.

What is an "appellation?"

An appellation is a legally designated winegrowing region. They are fairly large geographical areas divided into "subappellations" of various sizes For example, if a bottle label says "Cabernet Sauvignon Napa Valley," the grapes can come from anywhere in that area. But Napa is divided into subregions such as Yountville, Rutherford, Diamond Mountain, etc. And those may be further sectioned of into single vineyards or even blocks within vineyards. A label might say, "Napa Valley Diamond Mountain Miss Lil's Vineyard." Long story short, the more specific a wine is to a place, the finer – and more expensive – it's likely to be.

Does the shape of a wine glass really make a difference?

You bet. Wine glasses are made in various shapes to accomplish certain purposes. The deep broad bowl of a red wine glass, for instance, allows us to swirl the wine sufficiently to release the flavor and aroma components. They narrow toward the top to channel those aromas to the nose. And, since we taste flavors (sweet, salt, sour, and bitter) at different places on our tongues, different shapes direct what we drink to the right places. A white wine glass may be a bit taller and narrower, because of the more delicate nature of the flavors and aromas.

Why is wine stored in oak barrels?

Oak is to wine what spices and seasoning are to food. When winemakers decide to ferment or store wine in oak barrels, they're adding several important flavors and characteristics to the juice. People write whole books on what oak does to wine, but basically the flavors that the juice soaks up from the barrel are determined by where the wood comes from (France and America supply most of the barrels used in winemaking), and how the barrels are toasted on the inside. Wine barrels are made over flame, because heat makes the wood staves flexible so they can be bent into shape. Winemakers order barrels with light to heavy toast, depending on the flavors they want to extract. And then, of course, there's the decision of how long to leave the wine in barrels. Some Spanish wines stay in barrels for decades before they're released.

We're seeing a lot of arguments in print about wine bottles sealed with corks vs. screw tops. Which is better?

This is an argument that probably will never subside. Cork is, after all, an organic product: the bark of a certain type of oak tree. It breaks down over time, and worst of all, is subject to a fungus called TCA that robs the wine of its freshness or spoils it completely. Screw caps (the makers would prefer that we call them "twist-offs"), seal a bottle completely, and most likely can last forever.

Volumes have been written on this topic, but I'd say that wines you're planning on drinking over the next few years are perfectly fine with a "twist off." The more expensive wines will likely still be sealed with corks, at least for the immediate future.

Why do some wines give people headaches?
The culprit is histamines, which occur in grape skins. Some people (about 1% of the population) are sensitive to them. Most people who are sensitive to histamines get more headaches from red wines than from white. This is because red wine spends more time in contact with the skins during the fermentation process, and generates more histamines.

I've been invited to my first formal wine tasting, and am not sure what it's going to be like. I'd appreciate a few hints.
First, don't wear perfume or cologne. Sense of smell is over 85% of your sense of taste, and other aromas will be distracting. Second, eat before you go. Many events offer nibbles with the wines, but it's not enough. Third, don't be afraid to spit. Swallowing all the wines you try can send you home in a cab...or an ambulance. There should be spit buckets around the room. And ask questions. The people pouring the wines should be very knowledgeable, and they always welcome new aficionados. Enjoy.

When I was in Napa last summer, I saw people in the vineyards cutting bunches of grapes off the vines and dropping them on the ground. Why would growers waste the grapes like that?
Winegrowers "drop fruit" to increase the intensity of flavor in the remaining grapes on the vine. Too many bunches result in diluted, weak flavors. The fewer the bunches, the more intense the flavors in those that are left.

Why do some red wines make my mouth feel all dry and puckered?

Red wines have a component called "tannin," which comes from the skins, stems, and seeds of the grapes when they're crushed. Tannin is not a flavor; it's a critical wine component that provides structure. But tannic young red wines—and even older ones—may make you feel (in the words of WC Fields) like the Russian army marched through your mouth in stocking feet. Tannins diminish and integrate into other flavor components over time, which is why we cellar the big reds. You can also minimize that "puckery" feeling by decanting the wine, pouring it through an aerator, or accompanying it with salty foods.

How is natural wine different from organic wine?

Most organic wines, while made from organically grown grapes, may still be technologically or chemically manipulated during the winemaking process. In a way, all wine is organic, but not all organic wine is natural.

Once I open a bottle, how long will the wine keep?

Most everyday wines are at their best right away, and if you don't finish the whole bottle (never a problem at our house) you want to prolong the life of what's left. One method is a vacuum stopper, such as the Vac-u-Vin, which is what we generally use. The rubber bottle stoppers have a valve in them, and you remove the air from the stoppered bottle with a little hand pump. This generally allows the wine to stay fairly fresh for one or two days. If you just put the cork back in, the wine may last for a day or two, but every wine is different. Some have 2-3 day staying power, while others go downhill a lot faster.

I've heard that high-alcohol wines are not all that good. True or false?

Any winemaker will tell you that one of the most important qualities of a wine is balance. Are the fruit flavors, sugars, acids and alcohol levels in harmony? Does a wine feel "hot" on the palate because the alcohol content is too obvious? The fact is, many great wines have alcohol levels well north of 14%. Zinfandel, for example, is so "big" with bold fruit and sugar, that it can contain over 15% alcohol and you'd never know it. The riper the fruit at harvest, the bolder the fruit flavors will be, and, generally, the higher the alcohol content. If all the components of the wine are in balance, a higher alcohol percentage won't make a difference. Unless, of course, you drink half a bottle and try to operate heavy machinery.

I don't have a fancy wine cellar or anything. So what's the best way to store my wine?

The biggest enemies of wine are light, heat, and vibration. So definitely keep your bottles out of direct sunlight, and in a room where you don't keep the lights on all the time, like a back bedroom or study. You can store them at room temperature, and don't expose them to large variations in temperature. And don't put them in a cute little wine rack on top of the refrigerator. Vibration is a big no-no. If you have some really high quality wines, the bottom of a closet is usually a good choice.

I've seen professional wine critics put their noses all the way down inside a glass and take some sniffs. Why do wine tasters smell wine?
The aromas of a wine can give you a good hint about how it will taste – even where it was made and how old it might be. Besides, 85% of your sense of taste is actually smell. Most often, a wine's aromas (or "bouquet" or "nose") indicate what we're going to taste, but sometimes the taste will be very different.

Who in the world consumes the most wine?
Americans do, on a total volume basis. Between 2013 and 2016, wine consumption in the US increased 6.5%, while the French (in second place) drank 3.5% less. The rest of the Top Five: Italy, Germany, and China. On a per-capita basis, which may be more informative, 14 of the top 15 countries are in Europe, with Vatican City leading the list. The average Vatican resident drinks 54 liters a year, followed closely by Andorra, Croatia, and Slovenia. Americans drink about 10 liters per person per year. People in California, New York, and (no surprise) Florida drink the most wine per capita.

What part does yeast play in the making of wine?
No yeast, no wine. Yeast grows naturally on grape skins, and when it comes in contact with juice, fermentation occurs. This is when yeast digests sugar and spits out alcohol, though it's much more complicated than that. Problem is that naturally-occurring, or indigenous, yeast often isn't enough to complete the process, so winemakers add specially-grown strains during fermentation.

I've read that American oak is better than French for wine production. Is that true?

Oak is to winemaking what seasonings and spices are to cooking. A winemaker chooses American oak, which is loose-grained, to impart pronounced flavors of the wood, vanilla, toffee, and other components. Oak fermentation or ageing also helps soften tannins in red wines. If you want subtler flavors, you'd choose French oak. The tighter grain means wines won't absorb those components quite as readily. Note – it's also possible that the use of new oak promotes histamine levels in wine, which causes headaches in many people.

If a wine label says "Cabernet Sauvignon," is the wine in the bottle pure Cabernet, or are other grapes blended in?

Depending on the laws of the particular region or country, the bottle must contain between 75% and 85% of the named varietal. So if the label says "Cabernet Sauvignon," there can be up to 25% of other grapes blended in, and they don't have to be disclosed. Most times, blending improves a wine, adding, color, structure, or aroma. Places like France, Italy, and Spain don't list the name of the grape at all – just the name of the region the wine is from. For example, in the Southern Rhone, a red wine might consist of a blend of 10 to 13 different grapes, and the label will not let you know.

I'd like to take a few bottles of my favorite wines on an upcoming trip, but of course, airlines won't allow them on board. What's the best way to ship my wine as checked baggage?

There are several ways to solve this problem. First is to buy a piece of luggage made especially for the purpose, such as a SkyCrate, which is what I use. It holds up to 12 regular-sized bottles and is practically indestructible, but it's fairly large and mainly for professionals. If you order wine online, you can use the shipping box in which you receive your bottles. The styrofoam or "egg crate" inserts will protect them just fine. You can also tuck a few wine bottles in your regular luggage by sealing them in leakproof padded plastic sleeves like the Wine Skin, the VinniBag, or the Travelon inflatable pouch. These are all available at most wine stores, or online.

If I want to improve my wine tasting skills, what should I do?
The first thing is (you guessed it) drink a lot of wine. By that I mean sample widely. There are thousands of grapes and thousands of wines. Try different types – and different producers -- as much as you can. Then, "chew" the wine in your mouth—don't swallow right away. This brings the wine in contact with all the receptors on your tongue, and provides a fuller, more complete idea of the flavors. Last, taste with other people and compare your impressions. Just like we all see colors differently, we all have our individual sense of taste. Your friends might detect flavors you don't, and vice versa.

Is higher alcohol content any indication of higher quality in a wine?
Some wine grapes have enough fruit and structure to support high levels of alcohol. Zinfandel, for instance, is such a "big" wine that it can have over 15% alcohol

and you won't notice it. Other grapes, like Pinot Noir, are more subtle and delicate, and high alcohol content will feel "hot" on the palate. Regardless of the percentage of alcohol, winemakers strive to make sure all the elements of their wines, like acidity, fruit, and other components are always in balance.

How did the tradition of clicking glasses to "toast" begin?

Back in the old days, like the Middle Ages, it was common practice to poison the food and drink of your enemies. To show good faith, each person would pour a bit of their beverage into another person's cup, so that everyone was drinking pretty much the same thing. Over time, this process became shortened to a simple tap of one glass against the other.

I see the word "Reserve" on some American wine labels. What does it mean?

In the US, the word "reserve" has no special meaning. Winemakers can give any wine a reserve designation. However, in France, Italy, and other Old World countries, the term is legally regulated, and is used for wines that meet strict winemaking and aging requirements.

Many times when I order a glass of wine in a restaurant, I get what I think is a skimpy pour. Is there a standard number of ounces I should expect in my wine glass?

In the United States, a beverage portion is determined by how many grams of alcohol it contains. The "standard" number is 14 grams, which is found in one regular 12-oz. can of beer, or 5 oz. of table wine. Of course, the amount a particular bar or restaurant will pour is determined by their profit margins, but I think we should expect at least a 5 oz pour.

Recently, my husband and I attended a Wine tasting at a Renaissance Festival. I fell in love with a dessert wine called "Simply Psychodelic" and purchased a couple of bottles from a local winery. When we opened it at home and poured it into our glasses, we noticed right away a grainy "sugary" ring left by the wine. I have never seen this before and it made me raise my eyebrows. When we tasted it, it was much sweeter than we remembered. Is it common practice to add sugar to wine?

The sugary particles you saw were most likely crystals of tartaric acid -- cream of tartar. This sometimes crystallizes in wine, especially whites, and usually settles to the bottom of the bottle or sticks to the inside surface of the cork. It is harmless and no cause for concern. In the US, it is NOT legal to add sugar to wine, though some countries (like Germany) permit the practice. It's done during fermentation to increase alcohol content.

On a recent trip to Sonoma, we loved the peaceful views of the grapevines rolling off into the distance. But I have a feeling that life in the vineyard isn't as idyllic as it looks. Can you comment?

You're right. Grapevines face a multitude of hazards that keep winemakers up at night staring at the ceiling. In addition to pests like the glassy-winged sharpshooter and the root louse that spread deadly diseases, there's dry rot, powdery mildew, birds, raccoons and other critters, frost, hail…the list goes on. You may have seen vines covered with netting to keep the birds from eating the grapes that should rightfully go into the wine we enjoy. Growing wine grapes is not as attractive or relaxing as it looks from your hotel room balcony.

Is there any way to keep sparkling wines bubbly if we don't finish the whole bottle? Can you recommend any kind of stoppers that will keep it fresh?

The best stoppers I've found have a substantial inner ring made of rubber or plastic, and hinged clamps that come down on both sides and fasten to the ridge around the neck of the bottle. They usually keep bubblies in good condition for two or three days. However, they will not keep a bottle from leaking, so store leftover sparklers standing up.

All the Wine Wisdom You Need to Flabbergast Your Friends, Astound Your Associates, Amaze Your Acquaintances, and Dumbfound Your Dates.

PART VII
FINAL THOUGHTS

*A*s we used to say back in the Sixties,
it's been a long strange trip.

This journey through the world of wine has, as I mentioned at the outset, immeasurably enhanced our lives and our love for each other. It has taken us places we never would have gone otherwise.

It's been my pleasure to share that joy and excitement and discovery with many people over the years by teaching university courses, hosting wine seminars, charity wine events, private tastings, and working with other professionals to bring wine appreciation to a wider audience. I was the original Wine Director of the Southwest Florida Wine and Food Festival, which has grown to be one of the top charity wine events in America. I've also been retained to ghost write several books on a broad variety of topics, and am available to do that for anyone who's interested.

So. If you'd like to discuss a personal appearance for me to host or conduct any sort of wine function, speak to a group, or write a column for a publication (as I do now) I'd be delighted to receive your call. Or you may contact me if you'd like to be placed on my email list to receive notice of when my events take place and my articles are published.

I can be reached through the contact form on my website at www.winewhisperer.com, or by email at jerry@thewine-whisperer.com.

Here's to you!